Mappae mundi

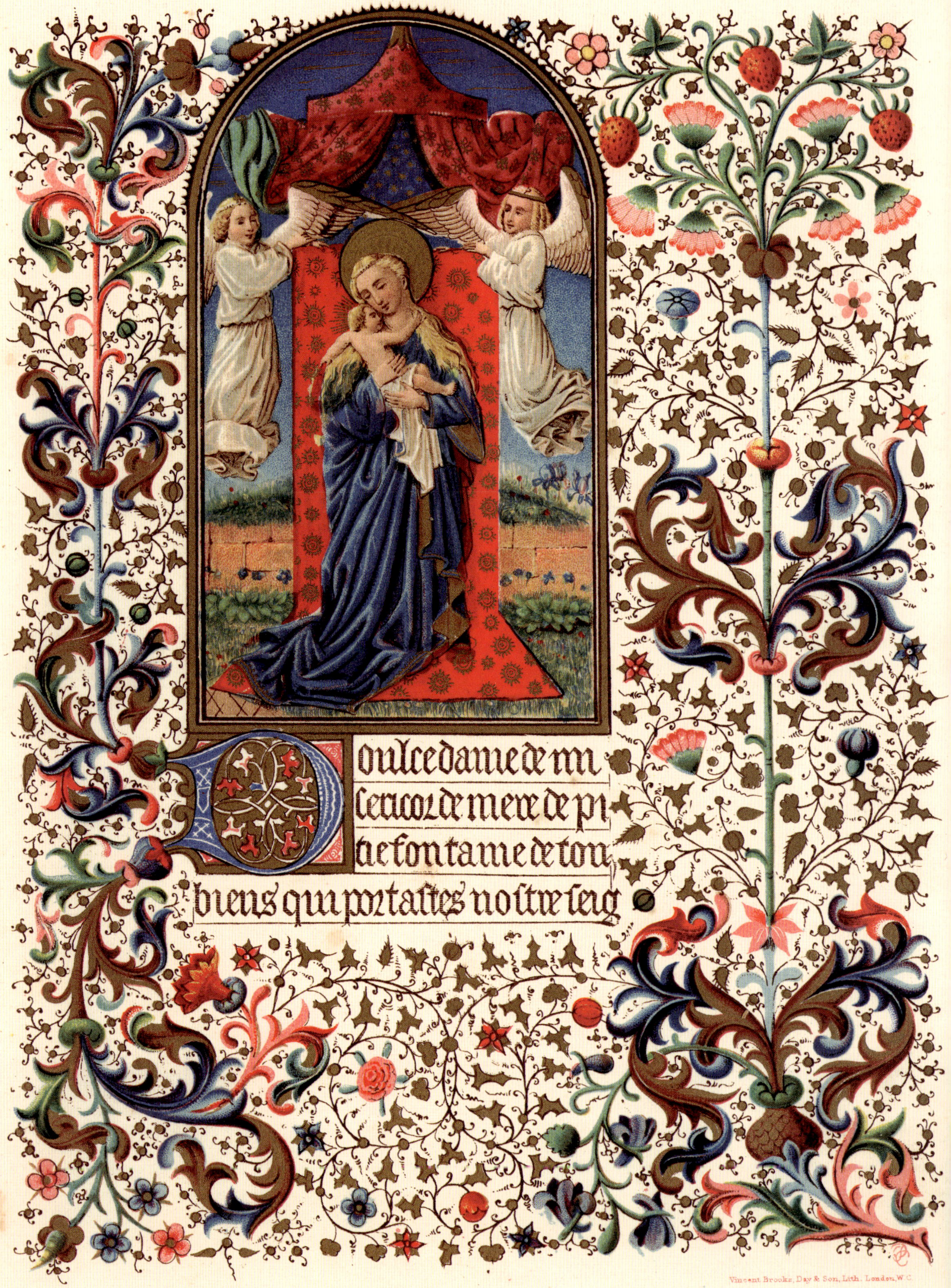

Vincent Brooks, Day & Son, Lith. London, W.C.

Mappae mundi

Bruce Peel Special Collections Library ✻ *February – April 2008*

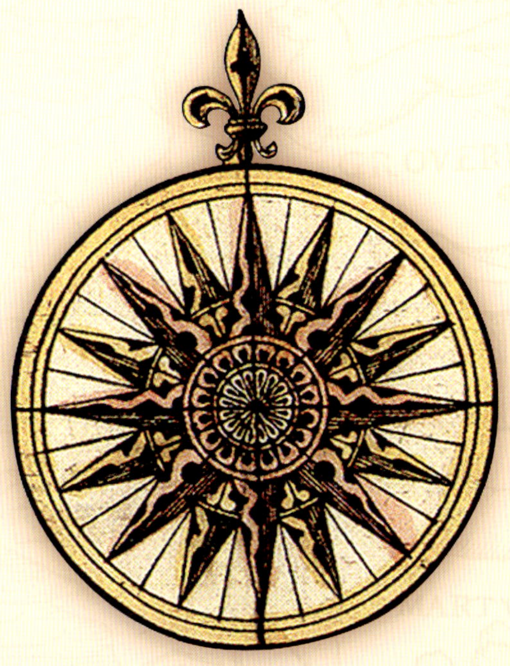

Representing the World and its Inhabitants in Texts, Maps, and Images in Medieval and Early Modern Europe

EXHIBITION AND CATALOGUE BY MICHAEL FOX AND STEPHEN R. REIMER
DEPARTMENT OF ENGLISH AND FILM STUDIES, UNIVERSITY OF ALBERTA

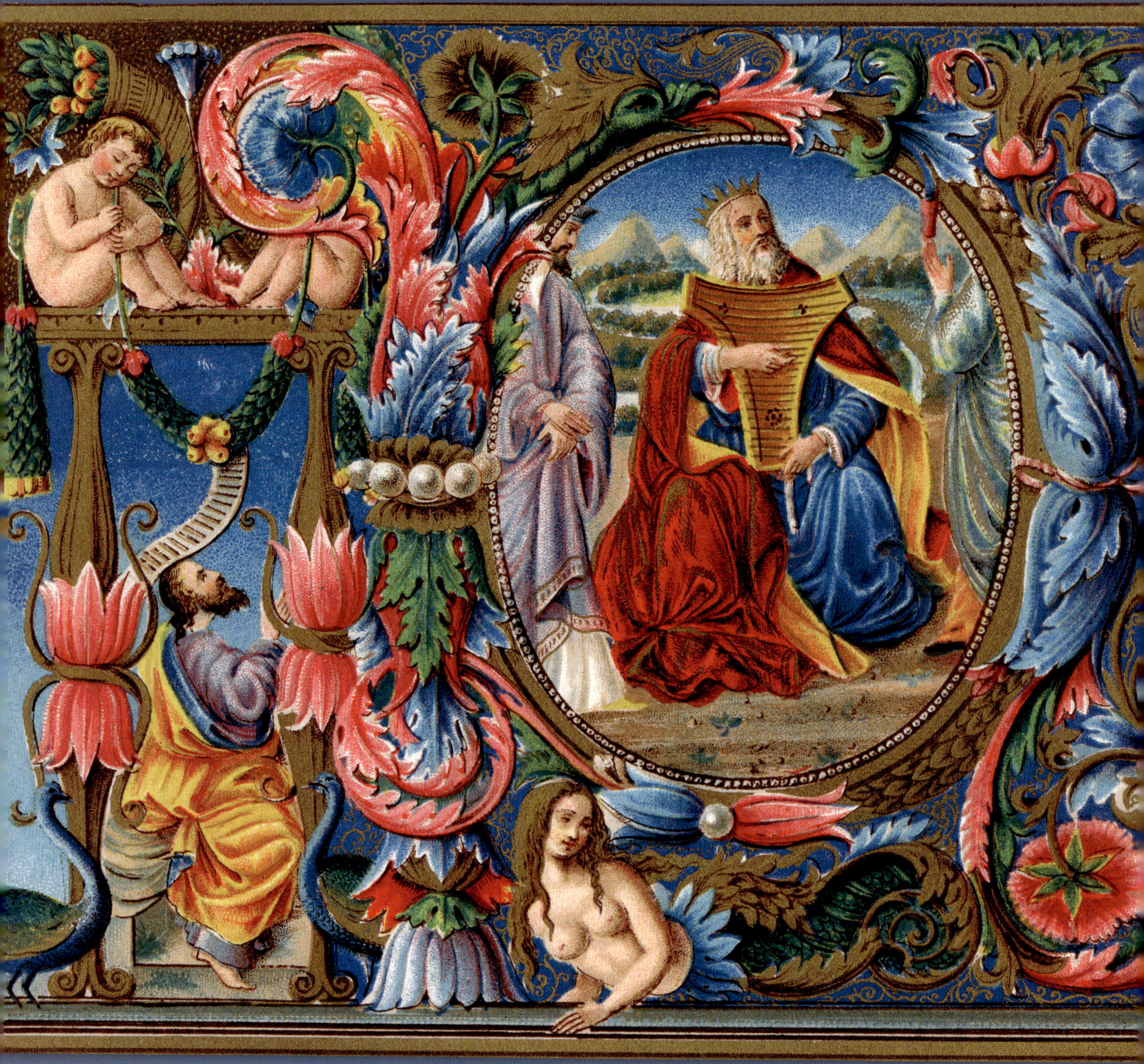

Foreword

In the fall of 2005, Angela Wesley Irwin, an MA student in the Department of English and Film Studies, passed away after a battle with cancer. In her memory, graduate students, faculty, and staff in the Department contributed to a fund to purchase a volume in her honour. Because of her love of cartography, it was decided that it ought to be a map, or to be a volume about maps. David L. Jones (map librarian in the William C. Wonders Map Collection) suggested the Zsolt Török new editions (Items 49, 51, and 59 of the four Török works in the exhibition) and also contributed the last requisite funds from his own budget. This exhibition, then, was initially conceived as an occasion to display the Török maps for the first time, and, through the generous and informed suggestions of Jeannine Green, Robert Desmarais, and David L. Jones, it grew to the full exhibition that you now see.

A second "seed" from which the exhibition grew was the recent acquisition of a copy of the colour facsimile of the Ellesmere manuscript of Chaucer's *Canterbury Tales*, and the link between Chaucer and maps suggested a theme of the world and its medieval representations, especially in terms of travel, pilgrims, and knowledge of the world's inhabitants, human, animal, and monstrous.

Along with the Török maps and the Ellesmere manuscript, a third treasure exhibited here, and one that demonstrates something of the current state of the art of replicating a medieval manuscript, is the reproduction of the *Book of Kells*, an early medieval copy, beautifully decorated, of the Gospels. The Bruce Peel Library's copy of the *Book of Kells* was given to the Library by the former Chancellor of the University, Sandy Mactaggart. Various other items in the exhibition were acquired by the Library through the generosity of donors, particularly the Department of History, the Friends of the Library, the Association of Professional Librarians of the University of Alberta, and two were purchased with Alberta Heritage Savings Trust Fund Library Development Grants. As scholars who use in our research and teaching facsimiles like the ones on exhibit here, we are grateful to these donors and to the University and its Libraries for making possible ready access to such primary research materials here at the University of Alberta.

Finally, we wish to thank Robert Desmarais, Peter Box, and Carol Irwin of the University of Alberta Libraries, who have been closely involved in the planning and preparation of the exhibition and the catalogue, and who have contributed much to both. We also wish to thank Linda Distad, our capable copyeditor, who saved us from many errors and inconsistencies; and Lara Minja of Lime Design, who made the catalogue a work of art.

MICHAEL FOX
STEPHEN R. REIMER

Contents

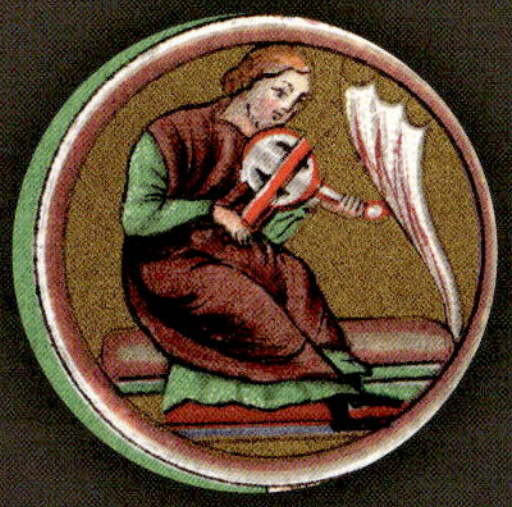

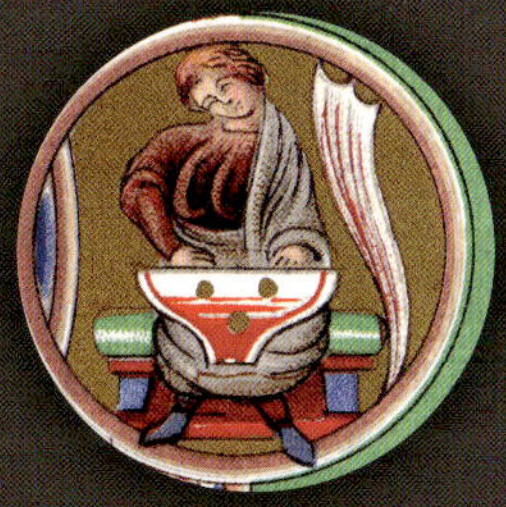

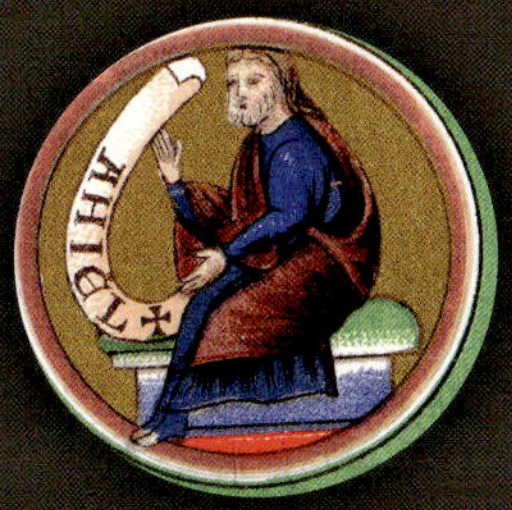

List of figures

Fig. 12: *The Trinity College Apocalypse* (Item 22; Cambridge, Trinity College Library, MS R.16.2), ff. 14v–15r: the seven-headed dragon of the Apocalypse.

Fig. 13: *Le psautier de Saint Louis* (Item 23; Paris, Bibliothèque nationale de France, Ms. latin 10525), ff. 9v–10r: the destruction of Sodom, and the Sacrifice of Isaac.

Fig. 14: *A Peterborough Psalter and Bestiary* (Item 25; Cambridge, Corpus Christi College, MS 53), f. 189r: in the historiated initial and in the miniature are images of the lion, in various situations described in the bestiary text.

Fig. 15: *Die Manessische Lieder-Handschrift* (Item 26; Heidelberg, Universitätsbibliothek, Cod. Pal. germ. 848), f. 71v: a lady uses a winch to bring her lover (Herr Kristan von Hamle) up to her room.

Fig. 16: *The Gough Map* (Item 30; Oxford, Bodleian Library, MS Gough Gen. Top. 16), detail: London and region.

Fig. 17: *The "Canterbury Tales": The New Ellesmere Chaucer Facsimile* (Item 36; San Marino, CA, Huntington Library, MS EL 26.C.9), ff. 153v–154r: the beginning of "The Tale of Melibee" with a portrait of Geoffrey Chaucer.

Fig. 18: *The Schedel World Map* (Item 49; Nuremberg, 1493): a new edition printed from an original woodcut by Zsolt Török.

Fig. 19: *Rosario de Juana la Loca* (Item 53; the Boston-Cambridge Rosary), ff. 2v–3r: the Visitation of Mary to Elizabeth.

Fig. 20: *The Grimani Breviary* (Item 55; Venice, Biblioteca Nazionale Marciana, MS Lat. XI 67 [7531]): Calendar image for February.

Fig. 21: *Olaus Magnus Carta marina 1539* (Item 58), detail: Biarmia, also known as Bjarmaland or Permia.

Fig. 22: John Speed, *The Counties of Britain* (Item 61), pp. 270–71: map of Ireland.

PICTURE CREDITS

We would like to thank the following libraries and publishers for permission to reproduce the images in this catalogue:

Cover: picture library of the Österreichische Nationalbibliothek / Austrian National Library; Figs. 1–3: ADEVA (Akademische Druck- u. Verlagsanstalt); Figs. 4–5: Durham Cathedral and its Library, and Rosenkilde and Bagger; Figs. 6–7: The Kungliga Biblioteket / National Library of Sweden, and Rosenkilde and Bagger; Fig. 8: ADEVA (Akademische Druck- u. Verlagsanstalt); Fig. 9: The Bodleian Library, University of Oxford; Fig. 10: ADEVA (Akademische Druck- u. Verlagsanstalt); Fig. 11: The Roxburghe Club; Fig. 12: The Master and Fellows of Trinity College Cambridge; Fig. 13: ADEVA (Akademische Druck- u. Verlagsanstalt); Fig. 14: The Roxburghe Club; Fig. 15: Universitätsbibliothek Heidelberg; Fig. 16: The Bodleian Library, University of Oxford; Fig. 17: The Huntington Library; Fig. 18: Professor Zsolt Török, Eötvös Loránd University; Fig. 19: Patrimonio Ediciones; Fig. 20: Thames and Hudson; Fig. 21: Professor Bosse Holmqvist (Stockholm University), and Lychnos; Fig. 22: Thames and Hudson.

wedding was furnished with guests.

And when the king came in to see the guests, he saw there a man which had not on a wedding garment, and he saith unto him, "Friend how camest thou in hither not having a wedding garment?" And he was speechless. Then said the king to the servants, "Bind him hand and foot, and take him away, and cast him into outer darkness; there shall be weeping and gnashing of teeth." For many are called but few are chosen."

Introduction

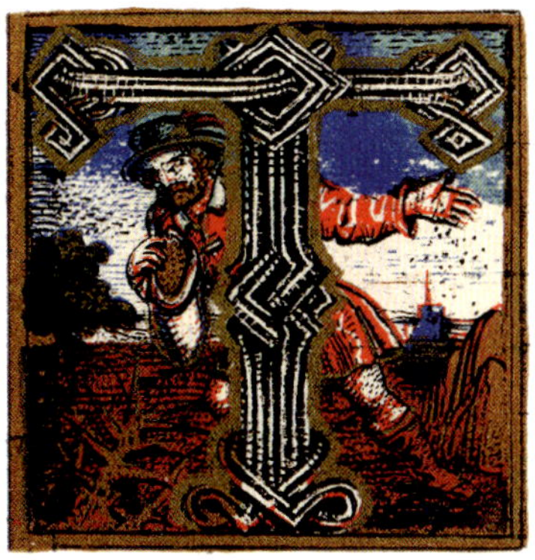

This exhibition showcases some of the treasures of the University of Alberta's Map and Special Collections, as well as other U of A libraries, particularly in terms of resources to aid in the study of the cultures of Medieval and Early Modern Europe. We have focused on "facsimiles" (though not all of the works included are technically facsimiles), and one of the ways to view the exhibition is in terms of the art of the facsimile, from early twentieth-century black-and-white photographs to twenty-first-century colour, digital photographs on CD-ROM. Further, an example such as the *Book of Kells* illustrates the impressive lengths to which some have gone to reproduce the details of primary sources, down to the worm holes in the pages, and to provide scholars with new kinds of facsimiles, full and accurate three-dimensional replicas of unique and often difficult to access originals. A second theme is ancient book production, from the papyrus roll through the medieval parchment codex, down to the modern printed book. In this narrative strand, one can examine developments in the techniques of book construction, in scribal hands, and in the decoration and illustration of books. A third theme is that of representations of the world and its inhabitants: humans, in their many activities and occupations; animals, wild and tame; monsters, to be feared especially in those parts of the world just beyond the boundary of the known. Here, too, a narrative line can be traced, in the evidence presented of the gradual, but ever so slow, growth in knowledge of the "other" parts of the world, a slow growth that is in such striking contrast to what has occurred in the last 400 years of exploration of the globe and even the solar system.

Though the origins of the printed word are to a certain extent impossible to recover, the first known ancestor of the modern

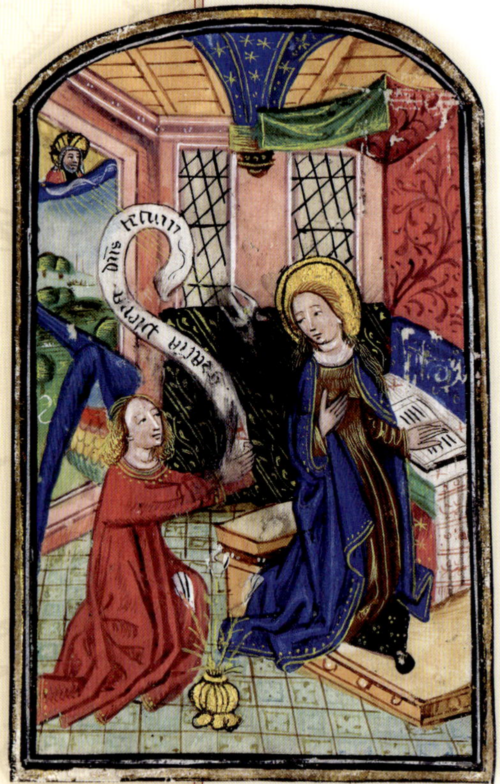

book is the papyrus roll (from which we get our modern word "paper"). The technology originated with the Egyptians, and was adopted first by the Greeks, then the Romans. Papyrus was made from the vertically ribbed pith of the triangular papyrus stalk. Strips of papyrus were first laid side-by-side, and then covered with a second layer at right angles. The papyrus sheets had to be stored in rolls in order to prevent the reeds from breaking apart. From the first century to the fourth, there was a gradual transition taking place from the roll to the codex (a form of the book with pages that could be turned) and from papyrus to parchment. These changes were partly due to the cumbersome nature of the roll, and partly to do with the spread of Christianity (and literacy) in the West, an environment which, on account of its dampness, was particularly hostile to the preservation of papyrus.

Strictly speaking, "parchment" is the skin of a sheep or goat, while "vellum" is a finer material, the skin from a calf, but the terms have often been used interchangeably, in the medieval period and even today. Generally, "vellum" designates a higher quality writing material, and "parchment" a writing surface of slightly lesser quality. Animal skins were usually prepared by being soaked in caustic calcium lye to loosen hair and remove fat. After being scraped clean, the skins were re-soaked, and then stretched on a frame to dry. The manner of the preparation of the skins, and the subsequent construction of the codex (how many pieces were sewn into each "quire"; which side of the skin faced which; how the skin was pricked or ruled to mark the area for writing; etc.) often tell us much about the period and location of each particular codex.

"Codex," then, is the technical name for the physical object made up of pages bound together along one edge, commonly called the "book," and the study of the production of the book is known as codicology. The word "manuscript" comes from the Latin *manuscriptus*, meaning "written by hand," and so has primarily to do with how the text was copied into the book. The particular study of the forms of handwriting, the "scripts," in manuscripts is known as "palaeography," and the study of changes in scripts can again tell us a great deal about the temporal and geographical origins of manuscripts. The history of scripts is too involved and lengthy to be sketched out here, but some of the technical names are included in the descriptions of the items in the catalogue. In the items on display, one can see evidence of a slow progression from Roman scripts to national hands, to Insular and Anglo-Saxon scripts, to Caroline minuscule, and finally to Protogothic and Gothic systems of scripts in the high and late Middle Ages. Within most script systems one can identify a hierarchy of scripts, meaning generally that scripts ranged from most formal to least formal. The Vatican Vergil (Item 2), for example, is written in "Rustic Capitals," an old Roman script just below the top script in the hierarchy, "Square Capitals," and just above "Old Roman Cursive," the script used in everyday documents and handwriting. The most popular and widespread hand of the early Middle Ages was "Caroline minuscule," which developed during the reign of Charlemagne in the late eighth century, and gradually was adopted even in England, at least in Latin manuscripts, by the middle of the tenth century. Norman and Angevin rule brought Protogothic script, and the Gothic system of scripts (which consists of a large number of different kinds of hands in a "complex hierarchy") remained in use for the rest of the Middle Ages, from about the end of the twelfth until the sixteenth century. From about 1400, in centres such as Rome and Florence, the Humanistic system of scripts developed and became a rival of Gothic scripts, or mixed with them, in certain regions of Italy and Western Europe.

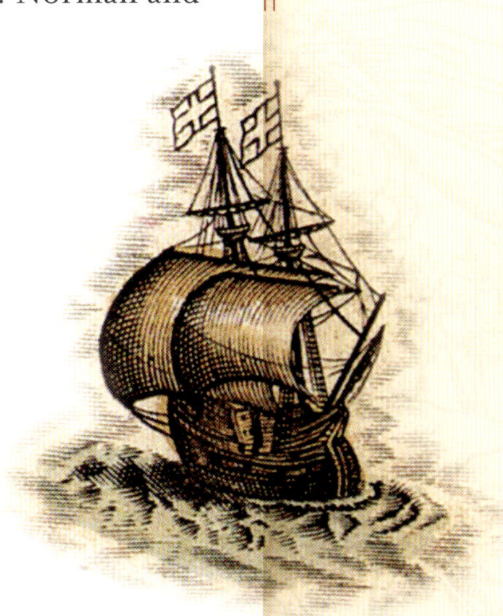

The vast majority of medieval manuscripts are quite plain and generally unremarkable records of texts; our exhibition includes a few of those, though they may be of importance for reasons beyond their plain appearance. When a medieval manuscript was decorated, however, it could become a quite glorious work of art. Since decoration added greatly to the cost of producing a book, it required significant justification, and in some cases this was relatively easy to find: books could be decorated lavishly in order to glorify God — while also casting some reflected glory upon the wealthy owner of the manuscript. Thus the books most likely to have decoration and illustration were sacred books, such as Gospels and Psalters (and the Apocalypse invites especially dramatic scenes), as well as liturgical books and prayer books (Antiphonals, Benedictionals, Breviaries, Books of Hours, etc.). There were also illustrations intended to serve pragmatic purposes: some books require illustration to clarify content, as in a book of beasts, for instance, or a book on surgical procedures, or a guide to medicinal herbs, and so forth. Over the course of time, the number of different types of books which were likely to attract illustrations grew to include chronicles and even fictive texts such as romances. The centres which set the fashions in the book arts changed from time to time in the later Middle Ages: in the twelfth and thirteenth centuries, for instance, Parisian artistic practices were imitated everywhere; in the fourteenth century, even Parisian artists began to look to Italy for models; and by the fifteenth century, especially with the rise in prestige of the Burgundian court, Flemish artists came to dominate and to be universally imitated.

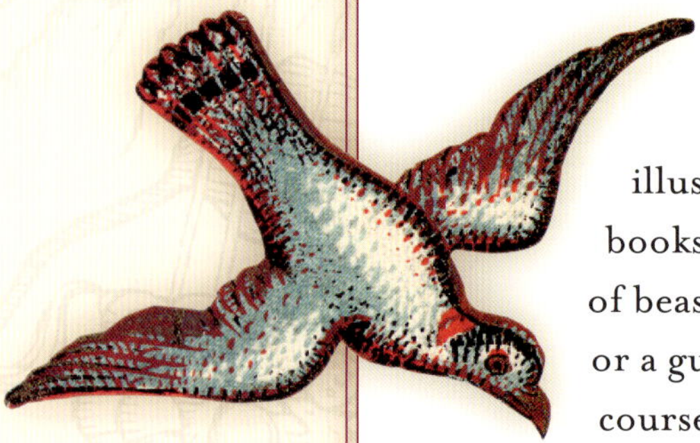

Among the types of sacred books that attracted elaborate decorative schemes and which will be encountered in our exhibition, the most sacred, of course, were Bibles, complete or incomplete, and a number of Gospel books and Psalters as well as an Apocalypse can be seen here. In the later Middle Ages, as book production came to serve not only the monasteries and universities, but also lay people, certain devotional practices among the laity gave rise to the production of certain kinds of books. In the twelfth and thirteenth centuries, for instance, a lay person who wished in private to imitate the devotional practices of monks and nuns (who had a daily round of eight "hours" each day and night at which they were to gather for prayers and the recitation of Psalms) might purchase a Psalter, the biblical book of the Psalms, and use it for private recitation. These Psalters were often elaborately decorated and illustrated, not generally with scenes directly illustrative of the topics of the Psalms, but with scenes of the Life of Christ, the lives of saints, and other sacred stories (sometimes in indirect "typological" or "thematic" relation to the particular Psalm which they accompany). Later in the thirteenth century, such Psalters gradually gave way to Books of Hours as the most common type of book of lay devotion. Besides personal Psalters and Books of Hours, we also include in the exhibition one Rosary, which is a highly simplified prayer book, offering fifteen devotional texts corresponding to the fifteen mysteries of the lives of Our Lord and Our Lady, each of which is accompanied by a Pater Noster and ten Ave Marias, to be counted on one's prayer beads while meditating upon the sacred scene represented in one or other of the pictures in the book.

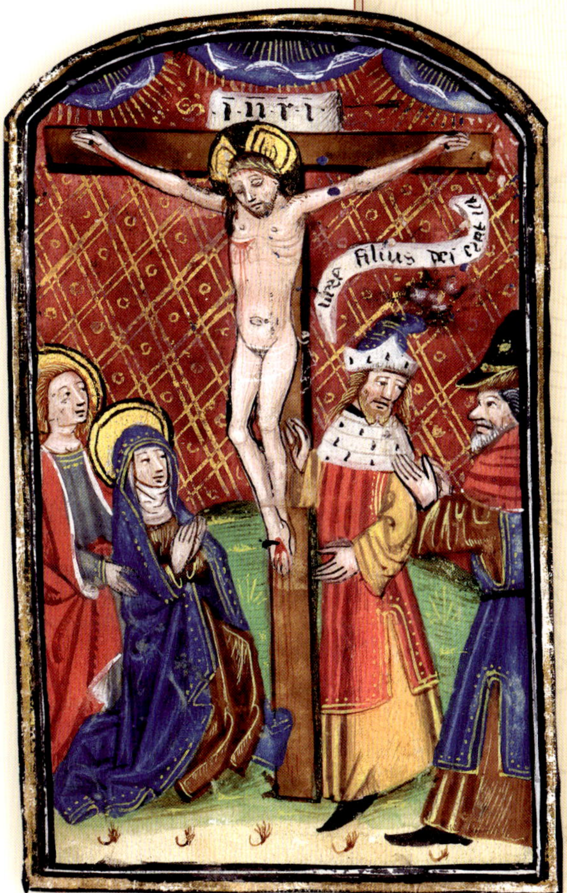

The Book of Hours, like the Psalter, imitates monastic devotional rituals by giving simplified forms of the "Offices" (collections of prayers and meditative readings), arranged according to the eight Hours of the monastic daily rituals. Besides the Offices, Books of Hours usually include a calendar showing the saints' days and high festivals, the seven penitential psalms, litanies, prayers to various saints, and readings from the Gospels. It is important to remember, though, that each Book was commissioned by and for a particular individual, and each Book of Hours is unique both in content and decoration. Books of Hours tended to be highly valued, given their religious and devotional purpose, and so, like the earlier Psalters, they tended to be written in fine calligraphic scripts and lavishly decorated. They are, then, "luxury" books, illustrating the best of medieval book production; they are also still highly prized and much sought after by collectors, and are visually appealing in an exhibition such as this.

The style of pictorial art changed over the course of the later Middle Ages, and this exhibition provides something of a narrative of increasing "realism" in pictures. This should not, however, be construed in progressivist terms, as some sort of development from simple-minded primitivism to sophisticated modernism. One should consider the possibility that early medieval people did not draw with perspective and a sense of "realistic" depth because they did not wish to do so, for it would not serve their artistic purposes. In Aristotelian terms, much of medieval art seems to be predicated on an idea that it is the "substance," the "essence," the "meaning" of a thing which is to be represented, not its "accidents"; the actual appearance of a person or thing is of much less importance than the "idea" of the person or thing. In medieval pictures, "important" people are, quite naturally, bigger than unimportant people; a king always wears a crown (even in bed) because it is the idea "king" that is being represented, not the actual behaviour of an actual person; a landscape may be suggested by a round hill and a stylized tree, with no attempt to make it "realistic"; the "light of heaven" will be represented by a golden backdrop to a scene, or a wallpaper-like pattern of colours, where a later artist would draw a naturalistic sky. In the fourteenth and

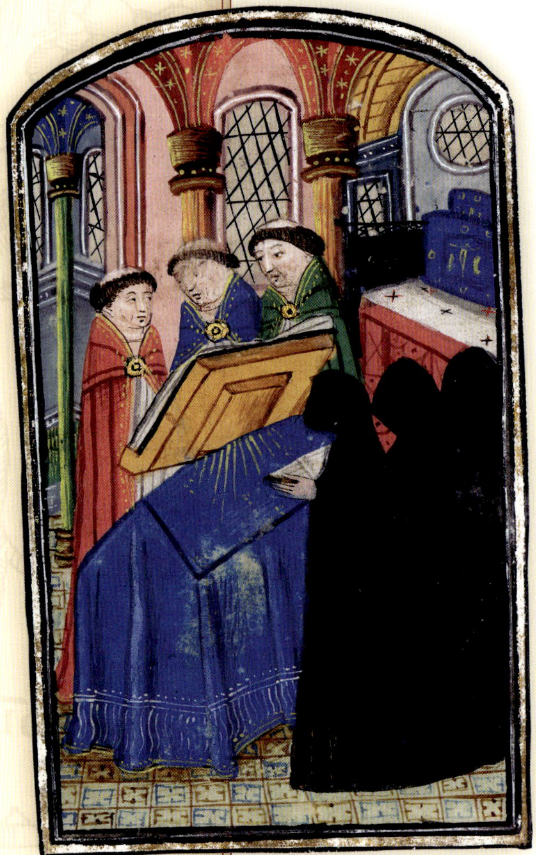

fifteenth centuries, however, we find much more interest being shown in providing distant prospects behind the central group of figures — as well as an increasing interest in the "third dimension" to be seen in a new emphasis upon the shading and modelling of rounded surfaces — and it is this shift towards a concern with "accidentals" that will lead, in the early modern period, to the development of techniques of perspective and other ways to enhance the "realism" of scenes. The gradual shift from the more "iconic" towards the more "realistic" in the pictorial art of the fourteenth and fifteenth centuries can be read (from a modern perspective) as "progress" towards "modernism." From another perspective, however, it could be understood as evidence that the religious significance of art, in its focus upon that which is "essential," was being lost, and was giving way to an increasing concern with the comparatively trivial, the merely decorative, the "accidentals" of mere appearances. We see something of this tension also in Chaucer, who portrays his pilgrims, when first we meet them, in terms of essences, of types — the thieving Miller, the crusading Knight, the perfect Parson, the shrewish Wife — though they do become more particularized and individual (some even acquire names) as we come to know them better. Thus, the tension between essence and accident, and between the generalizable and the particular, can be studied in the works of art presented here.

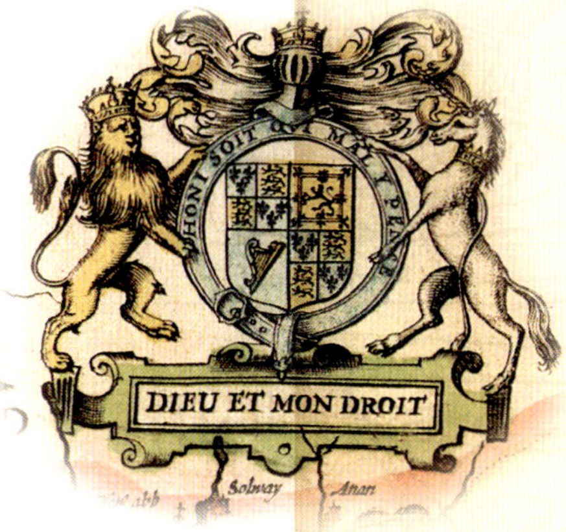

Maps, similarly, can illustrate how essence often trumped accident in medieval representations, for some of the maps seen here have much more to do with attempts to represent the world, not in terms of how it looks, but in terms of what it means. The Hereford Map, for instance, is a typical "O and T" (*orbis terrarum*) map, with its centre at Jerusalem, and its continents filled with images and texts that offer a full "narrative" of the history of the world and the biblical story of the Fall and Redemption of mankind. The Hereford Map hung for many centuries within Hereford Cathedral, where it could be seen and "read" by many, but it is also important to remember that this was the exception: maps were generally uncommon, not widely known or used. Most of the maps that survive from the Middle Ages were intended for a particular person or small group of people, and were "single purpose" or intended to communicate a single, limited idea about geographical space. There is, for instance (though it is not in this exhibition), a twelfth-century "bird's eye view" of Canterbury Cathedral and its adjacent priory, showing the underground water pipes and where they enter the various monastic buildings. There are itineraries for pilgrims, indicating the places along the routes to various shrines, or indicating the important places to visit once one arrives at Rome or in the Holy Land. There are portolan charts to aid navigation of bodies of water such as the Mediterranean Sea, by showing coastal outlines and including "rhumb lines" to help with calculating the direction one must take to get from one port to another. And from the thirteenth and fourteenth centuries there are several attempts to represent the British Isles, its geography and history, as in the maps that accompany the Chronicles of Matthew Paris, and the Gough Map (Item 30), a mid-fourteenth-century chart of England, Wales, Scotland, and the outlying islands, showing the principal cities, rivers, and highways.

It is important to remember that these maps were not diagrams of a "flat" earth, but intended as two-dimensional representations of a three-dimensional sphere. Since the time of Ptolemy, every educated person in the classical period and Middle Ages knew that the earth is a sphere, and that it could, theoretically, be circumnavigated. Rudolf Simek, for instance, in his contribution to *The Hereford World Map: Medieval World Maps and Their Context*, indicates that he has done a quite thorough search and has not found a single reference to a "flat" earth in European literature of the later Middle Ages: all references to the shape of the earth refer to it as a sphere. The idea that medieval people believed the earth to be flat is a nineteenth-century invention. Something like the Hereford Map, then, is not intended as an image of a flat "dish," but as a two-dimensional representation of half of a three-dimensional sphere.

The Hereford Map, like others, also attempts to represent some of the more exotic of the inhabitants of the sphere of the earth; if one looks closely at the parts of the map representing Asia and Africa, one can discover where Sciapods and other semi-human creatures are to be found (and Item 61 shows wild men and wild women living in Ireland). Medieval ideas about the "monstrous races" that exist in distant parts of the world were based on biblical stories of races of giants, and on classical myth: we find a cyclops in Homer's *Odyssey*; a Sphinx in the story of Oedipus, a race of warrior women, the Amazons, in the tales of Theseus; and Pliny's *Natural History* gives details of the races of giants, pigmies, dog-headed men, and men who are so monstrously "generous" that they offer their wives to every passing stranger. In the Middle Ages, such classical accounts were accepted without serious reservation, and not only maps but also bestiaries included accounts of the semi-human creatures in other parts of the world; indeed, theologians were known to have debates over whether such creatures were human enough to have souls and be in need of salvation. Furthermore, travellers' tales, such as the *Travels of Marco Polo* or the *Travels of Sir John Mandeville*, include stories of encounters with such creatures in the Far East, thus offering "eye-witness" verification of their existence.

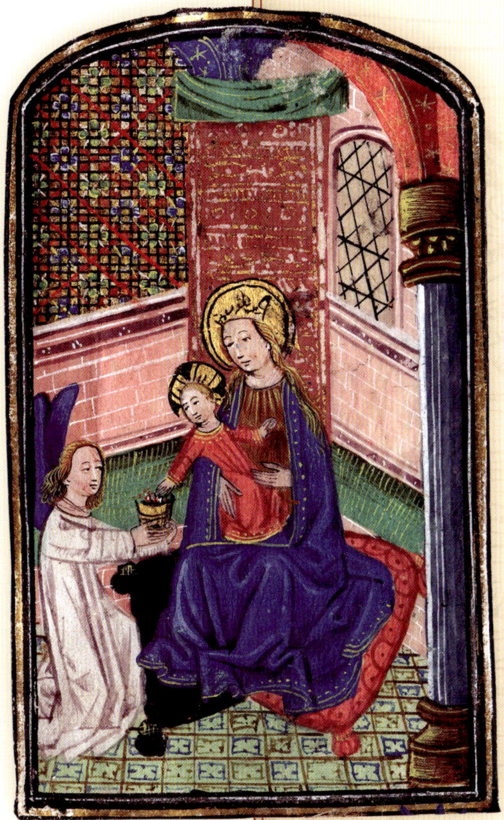

We have chosen to arrange the items in this catalogue according to chronology, although other arrangements (by genre, style, or theme) would be obvious alternatives with much to commend them. The principal justification for the chronological arrangement is that historical developments from one period to the next are the more readily apparent. One of the grand narratives suggested by this exhibition, then, has to do with the growth and changes in knowledge of the world and its inhabitants. Again, it is important to remember that the "flat earth" was not part of the medieval belief system. But another misconception has been the idea that medieval Europeans as a whole were severely circumscribed in terms of travel, and that it was a very rare thing for a medieval person to wander beyond a very short distance from home, yet Chaucer's Wife of Bath tells us that she has been to Rome, Spain, and Jerusalem. She is wealthy, of course, and she is exceptional in other ways, but still her "wanderings" serve as a corrective to the idea that medieval Europeans knew little of the world beyond their own village. Nevertheless, it is still true that European knowledge of the non-European world was very slow to develop, and the world of Pliny, Ptolemy, and Aristotle was still basically the same world of Shakespeare and Milton, of Columbus and Magellan, and there is a great contrast between the speed with which the world was explored in the last few centuries and the relative dearth of exploration (with some interesting exceptions) in the millennia before that.

Another of the narratives told by this exhibition is that of the book and its history. Again, one should not view this exhibition as a progressivist narrative of how the technologies of the book and the map have moved, slowly but steadily, towards "sophistication" and "modernization." Rather, we hope to have illustrated how these technologies are adapted, in different times and different places, to different sets of cultural values, to different social needs. Further, we hope that, amidst the range of "other" ways of representing the world that we have shown here, there is also a sense of what remains constant and familiar: for all their "otherness" and strangeness, the objects in this exhibition can be recognized as the ancestors of our own maps and books.

A short bibliography follows, offering suggestions for additional reading on the key ideas around which this exhibition is organized. Other books and articles that provide additional information about specific items in the exhibition will be listed at the end of the relevant entry in the catalogue. ❊

Suggestions for further reading

THE MEDIEVAL BOOK

Braswell, Laurel Nichols. *Western Manuscripts from Classical Antiquity to the Renaissance: A Handbook*. New York and London: Garland Publishing, 1981.

Brownrigg, Linda L., ed. *Medieval Book Production: Assessing the Evidence; Proceedings of the Second Conference of the Seminar in the History of the Book to 1500, Oxford, July 1988*. Los Altos Hills, CA: Anderson-Lovelace / The Red Gull Press, 1990.

Chaytor, H.J. *From Script to Print: An Introduction to Medieval Literature*. Cambridge: Cambridge University Press, 1945.

Glaister, Geoffrey Ashall. *Glaister's Glossary of the Book: Terms used in Papermaking, Printing, Bookbinding and Publishing, with Notes on Illuminated Manuscripts and Private Presses*. 2nd ed. Berkeley: University of California Press, 1979. (Reissued as *The Encyclopedia of the Book*, New Castle, DE: Oak Knoll Press, 1996 and 2001.)

Griffiths, Jeremy, and Derek Pearsall, eds. *Book Production and Publishing in Britain, 1375–1475*. Cambridge Studies in Publishing and Printing History. Cambridge: Cambridge University Press, 1989.

Gruys, A., and J.P. Gumbert, eds. *Codicologica: Towards a Science of Handwritten Books / Vers une science du manuscrit / Bausteine zur Handschriftenkunde*. 5 vols. Litterae textuales. Leiden: E.J. Brill, 1976–1980.

Manion, Margaret M., and Bernard J. Muir, eds. *Medieval Texts and Images: Studies of Manuscripts from the Middle Ages*. Chur, Reading, Paris, Philadelphia, Tokyo, and Melbourne: Harwood Academic Publishers; Sydney: Craftsman House, 1991.

Walther, Ingo F., and Norbert Wolf. *Codices illustres: The World's Most Famous Illuminated Manuscripts, 400 to 1600*. Köln and London: Taschen Verlag, 2001.

SCRIPTS

Bischoff, Bernhard. *Latin Palaeography: Antiquity and the Middle Ages*. Trans. Dáibhí O. Cróinín and David Ganz. Cambridge: Cambridge University Press, in association with the Medieval Academy of Ireland, 1990.

Bishop, T.A.M. *English Caroline Minuscule*. Oxford Palaeographical Handbooks. Oxford: Clarendon Press, 1971.

Boyle, Leonard E. *Medieval Latin Palaeography: A Bibliographical Introduction*. Toronto Medieval Bibliographies 8. Toronto: University of Toronto Press, in association with the Centre for Medieval Studies, 1984.

Brown, Michelle P. *The British Library Guide to Writing and Scripts: History and Techniques*. The British Library Guides. London: British Library, 1998.

———. *A Guide to Western Historical Scripts from Antiquity to 1600*. London: British Library, 1990.

Brown, T. Julian. *A Palaeographer's View: The Selected Writings of Julian Brown*. Ed. Janet Bately, Michelle P. Brown, and Jane Roberts. Pref. Albinia C. de la Mare. London: Harvey Miller Publishers, 1993.

Derolez, Albert. *The Palaeography of Gothic Manuscript Books: From the Twelfth to the Early Sixteenth Century*. Cambridge Studies in Palaeography and Codicology 9. Cambridge: Cambridge University Press, 2003.

Drogin, Marc. *Medieval Calligraphy: Its History and Technique*. Montclair, NJ: Allanheld and Schram, 1980.

Lowe, Elias Avery, ed. *Codices latini antiquiores: A Palaeographical Guide to Latin Manuscripts Prior to the Ninth Century*. 12 vols. Oxford: Clarendon Press, 1934–1972.

Parkes, M.B. *English Cursive Book Hands, 1250–1500*. Oxford Palaeographical Handbooks. Oxford: Clarendon Press, 1969.

Wardrop, James. *The Script of Humanism: Some Aspects of Humanistic Script, 1460–1560*. Oxford: Clarendon Press, 1963.

Wright, Cyril Ernest. *English Vernacular Hands from the Twelfth to the Fifteenth Centuries*. Oxford Palaeographical Handbooks. Oxford: Clarendon Press, 1960.

MANUSCRIPT ILLUMINATION

Alexander, J.J.G. *Medieval Illuminators and Their Methods of Work*. New Haven: Yale University Press, 1992.

Backhouse, Janet. *The Illuminated Page: Ten Centuries of Manuscript Painting in the British Library*. London: British Library, 1997.

Brown, Michelle P., and Scott McKendrick, eds. *Illuminating the Book: Makers and Interpreters: Essays in Honour of Janet Backhouse*. British Library Studies in Medieval Culture. London: British Library, 1998.

Calkins, Robert G. *Illuminated Books of the Middle Ages*. Ithaca, NY: Cornell University Press, 1983.

Camille, Michael. *Image on the Edge: The Margins of Medieval Art*. Essays in Art and Culture. Cambridge, MA: Harvard University Press, 1992.

De Hamel, Christopher. *A History of Illuminated Manuscripts*. Oxford: Phaidon Press, 1986.

Marks, Richard, and Nigel Morgan. *The Golden Age of English Manuscript Painting, 1200–1500*. New York: George Braziller, 1981.

McKendrick, Scot. *Flemish Illuminated Manuscripts, 1400–1550*. London: British Library, 2003.

Pächt, Otto. *Book Illumination in the Middle Ages: An Introduction*. Trans. Kay Davenport. Pref. J.J.G. Alexander. London: Harvey Miller Publishers; Oxford and New York: Oxford University Press, 1986.

Westwood, J.O., and Iain Zaczek. *The Art of Illuminated Manuscripts: Illustrated Sacred Writings*. Rev. ed. London: Studio Editions / Random House UK, 1996.

DEVOTIONAL BOOKS

Backhouse, Janet. *Illumination from Books of Hours*. London: British Library, 2004.

Gameson, Richard, ed. *The Early Medieval Bible: Its Production, Decoration and Use*. Cambridge Studies in Palaeography and Codicology. Cambridge: Cambridge University Press, 1994.

Henderson, George. *From Durrow to Kells: The Insular Gospel-books, 650–800*. London: Thames and Hudson, 1987.

Henisch, Bridget Ann. *The Medieval Calendar Year*. University Park: Pennsylvania State University Press, 1999.

Hughes, Andrew. *Medieval Manuscripts for Mass and Office: A Guide to Their Organization and Terminology*. Toronto: University of Toronto Press, 1982.

Penketh, Sandra. "Women and Books of Hours." In *Women and the Book: Assessing the Visual Evidence*. Ed. Jane H.M. Taylor and Lesley Smith. British Library Studies in Medieval Culture. London: British Library, 1997. 266–280.

Wieck, Roger S. *Painted Prayers: The Book of Hours in Medieval and Renaissance Art*. New York: George Braziller, in association with the Pierpont Morgan Library, 1997.

MEDIEVAL MAPS

Delano-Smith, Catherine, and Roger J.P. Kain. *English Maps: A History*. British Library Studies in Map History 2. London: British Library, 1999.

Edson, Evelyn. *Mapping Time and Space: How Medieval Mapmakers Viewed Their World*. British Library Studies in Map History 1. London: British Library, 1997.

Harvey, P.D.A., ed. *The Hereford World Map: Medieval World Maps and Their Context*. London: British Library, 2006.

——. *Medieval Maps*. London: British Library, 1991.

Hiatt, Alfred. "Mapping the Ends of Empire." In *Postcolonial Approaches to the European Middle Ages: Translating Cultures*. Ed. Ananya Jahanara Kabir and Deanne Williams. Cambridge Studies in Medieval Literature 54. Cambridge: Cambridge University Press, 2005. 48–76.

THE MONSTROUS IN THE MEDIEVAL WORLD

Baxter, Ron. *Bestiaries and Their Users in the Middle Ages*. Stroud, Gloucestershire: Alan Sutton Publishing; London: Courtauld Institute, 1998.

Bildhauer, Bettina, and Robert Mills, ed. *The Monstrous Middle Ages*. London: British Library; Toronto: University of Toronto Press, 2003.

Bovey, Alixe. *Monsters and Grotesques in Medieval Manuscripts*. Medieval Life in Manuscripts. London: British Library, 2002.

Friedman, John Block. *The Monstrous Races in Medieval Art and Thought*. Cambridge, MA: Harvard University Press, 1981.

Le Goff, Jacques. "The Marvelous in the Medieval West." In *The Medieval Imagination*. By Jacques Le Goff. Trans. Arthur Goldhammer. Chicago and London: University of Chicago Press, 1988. 27–44.

Williams, David. *Deformed Discourse: The Function of the Monster in Mediaeval Thought and Literature*. Exeter: University of Exeter Press; Montreal: McGill-Queen's University Press, 1996.

Catalogue

1. The Book of Proverbs, in Coptic

Manuscript: Berlin, Staatsbibliothek, MS Orient. oct. 987.
Produced in the 3rd or 4th century.
Papyrus; 43 leaves; 13 x 12.4 cm.
Facsimile on display: *Proverbien-Kodex / The Book of Proverbs (Codex)*. Ed. Alexander Böhlig. Leipzig: VEB Edition Leipzig, 1963.

WHILE THE PRESERVATION of papyrus documents is relatively rare, at least in comparison with those written on parchment or vellum, Berlin, Staatsbibliothek, MS Orient. oct. 987 (known as the Berlin Codex) is — as a complete book, preserved even with its binding — highly unusual. Papyrus documents were originally in the form of rolls, but this manuscript, as a book bound in one gathering, is one of the first papyrus documents in the transition from roll to codex. The text is the Old Testament Book of *Proverbs*, and it may be one of the oldest preserved books written in the Akhmîm dialect of Coptic, probably translated from Sahidic, another Coptic dialect, in an attempt to claim for Akhmîmic the status of a "literary language." The foundation of the Coptic text, however, would have been the Greek text of the Septuagint. *Proverbs* was an extremely important book in Coptic literature, as versions of the book exist in three dialects, and it is often cited.

The opening on display is the beginning of *Proverbs*. Even in facsimile, one can note the ribbed stalks of the papyrus and see the major differences between papyrus and parchment as writing surfaces. ✻

Böhlig, Alexander. *Der achmimische Proverbientext nach Ms. Berol. orient. oct. 987*. Studien zur Erforschung des christlichen Ägyptens, Heft 3. Munich: R. Lerche, 1958.

———. *Untersuchungen über die Koptischen Proverbientexte*. Stuttgart: W. Kohlhammer, 1936.

2. The Vatican Vergil

Manuscript: Vatican City, Biblioteca Apostolica Vaticana, Cod. Vat. lat. 3225.
Produced ca. 400 in the vicinity of Rome.
Parchment; 75 leaves (fragmentary); 22 x 19.7 cm.
Illustrated throughout (approximately fifty miniatures in all).
Script: "expert normative Rustic capitals in scriptura continua."
Facsimile on display: *Vergilius Vaticanus: vollständige Faksimile-Ausgabe im Originalformat des Codex Vaticanus Latinus 3225 der Biblioteca Apostolica Vaticana*. Ed. David H. Wright. Graz: Akademische Druck- u. Verlagsanstalt, 1984.

THIS MANUSCRIPT has been described by the editor of this facsimile, David H. Wright, as "deservedly the most famous illustrated manuscript to have survived from classical antiquity" (11). The manuscript is unfortunately more a series of fragments than any kind of continuous text. Wright estimates that we have 75 out of what must have been a text of some 439 leaves. The surviving leaves contain portions of Vergil's most famous work, the *Aeneid*, as well as portions of the *Georgics*. Written and illustrated in Rome sometime between 370 and 430, the manuscript remained in Italy for some time before the first half of the ninth century, when there is evidence that it was in Tours, a major centre in the Carolingian era, and where it probably remained (at least in France) until repatriated to Italy at some point in the fifteenth century. By the early sixteenth century, its illustrations were being adapted by Italian artists, the first of which is Raphael in 1514. The manuscript was bequeathed to the Vatican in 1600.

The opening on display, ff. 48v–49r (picturae 34 and 35), shows two images illustrating Book VI of the *Aeneid*, along with several fragments of text (VI.414–16, 417–23, 491–93 and 494–98). The illustrations depict Aeneas and the Sibyl as they pacify Cerberus (pictura 34) and then as they meet Deiphobos, and Tisiphone seated, guarding the gate of Tartarus (pictura 35). ❋

Wright, David H. *The Vatican Vergil: A Masterpiece of Late Antique Art*. Berkeley: University of California Press, 1993.

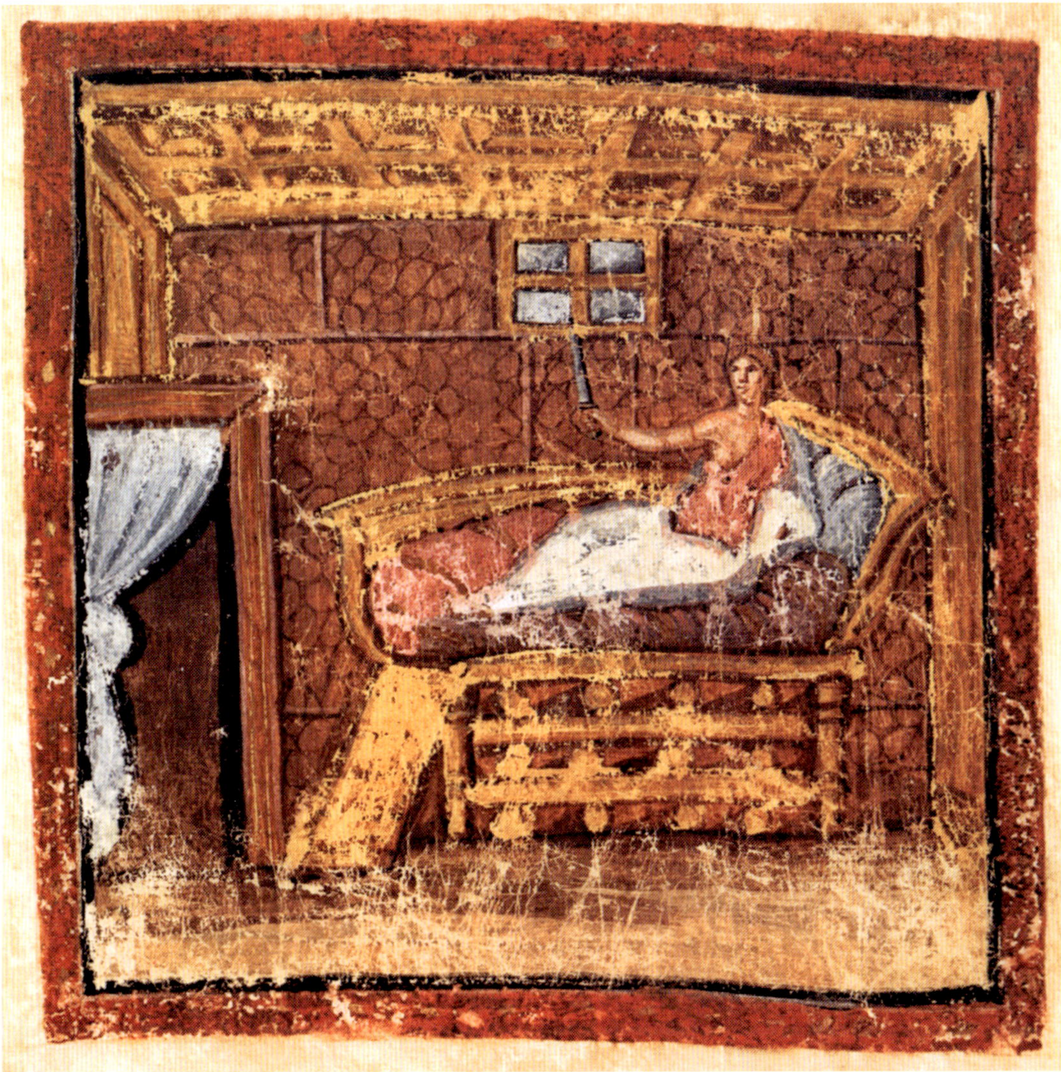

Fig. 1

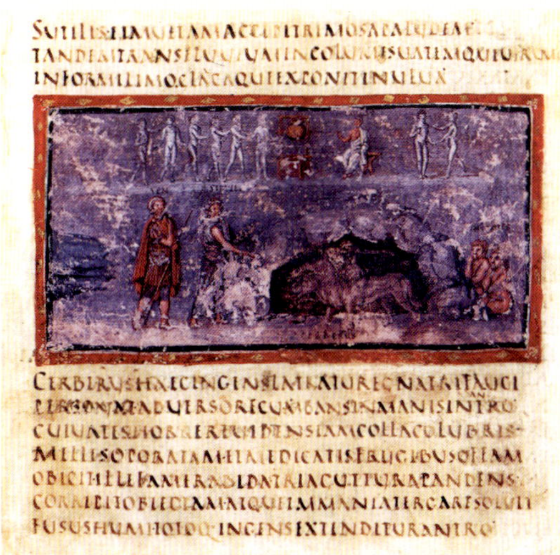

Fig. 2

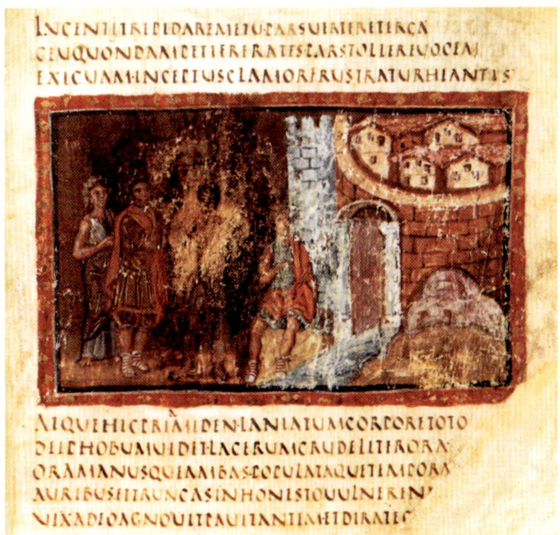

Fig. 3

3. The Durham Gospels

Manuscript: Durham, Cathedral Library, MS A.II.17, with an additional leaf, Cambridge, Magdalene College, Pepysian MS 2981 (19).
Produced in the late 7th or early 8th century, probably in Northumbria, perhaps at Lindisfarne.
Parchment; 108 leaves; 34.4 x 26.5 cm.
Decoration: many decorated initials; three full-page decorations.
Script: Insular half-uncial.
Principal contents:
Ff. 2r–38v: John 1:1–19:33 (missing 6:53–7:26).
Ff. 40r–69v: Mark 1:12–16:14 (missing 14:66–15:17).
Ff. 70r–102v: Luke 1:8–22:2 (missing 2:22–3:11 and 8:37–12:42).
Facsimile on display: *The Durham Gospels, Together with Fragments of a Gospel Book in Uncial: Durham, Cathedral Library, MS A.II.17*. Ed. Christopher D. Verey, T. Julian Brown, and Elizabeth Coatsworth. Early English Manuscripts in Facsimile 20. Copenhagen: Rosenkilde and Bagger, 1980.

TRADITION HAS IT that Pope Gregory (ca. 540–604), upon seeing some Anglo-Saxon youths for sale in the marketplace in Rome, was immediately able to divine from their appearance and race, the name of their territory, and the name of their king that they were innately suited for conversion to Christianity. Unable to go himself, however, he sent St. Augustine on the mission, and Augustine landed in Kent in 597. Though we cannot be certain what Augustine brought along, it seems likely that two manuscripts of the Gospels made the trip, as two sixth-century Italian uncial books have long been associated with Canterbury (Cambridge, Corpus Christi College Library, MS 286, and Oxford, Bodleian Library, MS Auct. D.II.14). Within a hundred years of Augustine's arrival, though, the Anglo-Saxons were producing their own versions of the Gospels. The earliest insular gospel manuscript is a series of fragments at Durham (Durham, Cathedral Library, MSS A.II.10, C.II.13, and C.III.20), probably written by an Irish scribe in Northumbria in the seventh century. That the scribe might have been Irish reminds us that the Irish were already Christian in the sixth century, and had in fact been instrumental in establishing monasteries both before and after the coming of Augustine, including, most famously, the monastery at Iona off the west coast of Scotland (founded by Columba in 563) and the monastery of Lindisfarne in Northumbria (founded by Aidan in 635). It is likely that both Augustine's mission and the efforts of the Irish are responsible for the spread of Christianity in England, at least to some degree, and for the style of those luxurious gospel manuscripts which survive.

Northumbria was a prominent centre in the seventh century, and many further Gospel manuscripts (and another famous manuscript of the complete Bible, the Codex Amiatinus) were written in Lindisfarne and Bede's twin monasteries of Wearmouth-Jarrow. The "golden age" of insular gospel manuscript production, therefore, might be said to have lasted from the late seventh century until the time of the production of the Book of Kells (ca. 800). Perhaps as a result of Viking incursions and a general decline in Latin learning, we have no surviving gospel manuscripts from the ninth century until early in the tenth. Toward the end of the Anglo-Saxon period, however, the production of gospel manuscripts reaches its height, as perhaps nineteen copies survive from the period between 990 and 1066.

Durham, Cathedral Library A.II.17 is, in fact, a composite volume, which means that it is comprised of what were formerly two separate manuscripts, both of which were Latin gospel books of the late seventh or early eighth century. Ff. 2–102 are the true "Durham Gospels" written in insular half-uncial and decorated in the tradition of other deluxe gospel books such as the Book of Durrow, the Lindisfarne Gospels, and the Book of Kells. Ff. 103–11, on the other hand, often referred to as "The Uncial Leaves," are in fact written in uncial, more like the hand of the famous Codex Amiatinus, a complete Bible from Wearmouth-Jarrow.

The opening on display begins with the second verse of the first chapter of the gospel of John (1:2) ("hoc erat in principio apud Deum," etc.). ✻

McGurk, Patrick. *Latin Gospel Books from AD 400 to AD 800*. Les publications de scriptorium 5. Paris: Éditions Érasme, 1961.

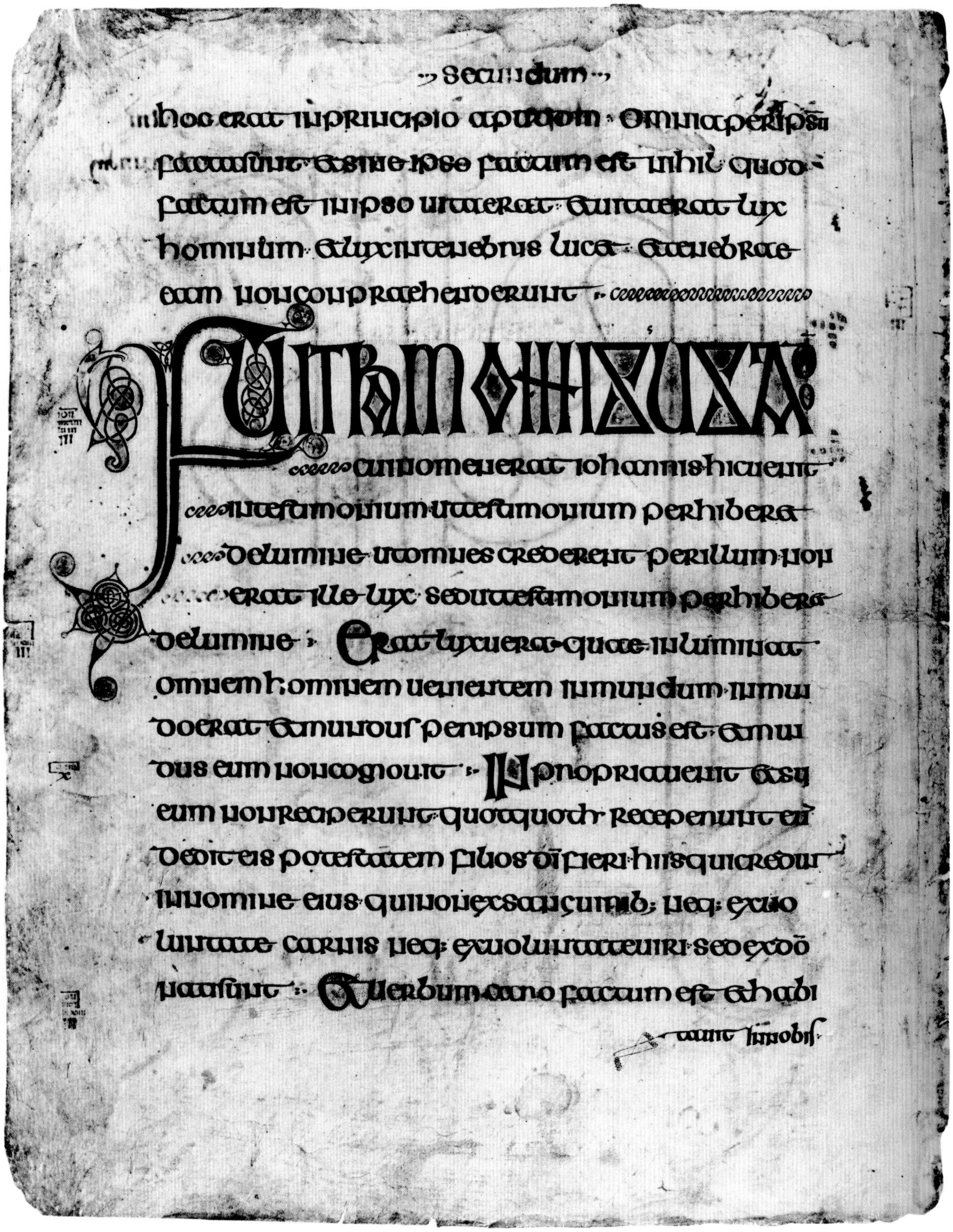
Secundum
hoc erat in principio apud dominum · omnia per ipsum
facta sunt et sine ipso factum est nihil quod
factum est in ipso uita erat · et uita erat lux
hominum · et lux in tenebris lucet · et tenebrae
eam non conprehenderunt
FUIT HOMO MISSUS A
cui nomen erat iohannis hic uenit
in testimonium ut testimonium perhiberet
de lumine ut omnes crederent per illum non
erat ille lux sed ut testimonium perhiberet
de lumine · Erat lux uera quae inluminat
omnem hominem uenientem in mundum · in mun
do erat et mundus per ipsum factus est et mun
dus eum non cognouit · In propria uenit et sui
eum non receperunt quotquot autem receperunt eum
dedit eis potestatem filios dei fieri his qui credunt
in nomine eius qui non ex sanguinibus neque ex uo
luntate carnis neque ex uoluntate uiri sed ex deo
nati sunt · Et uerbum caro factum est et habi
tauit in nobis

Fig. 4

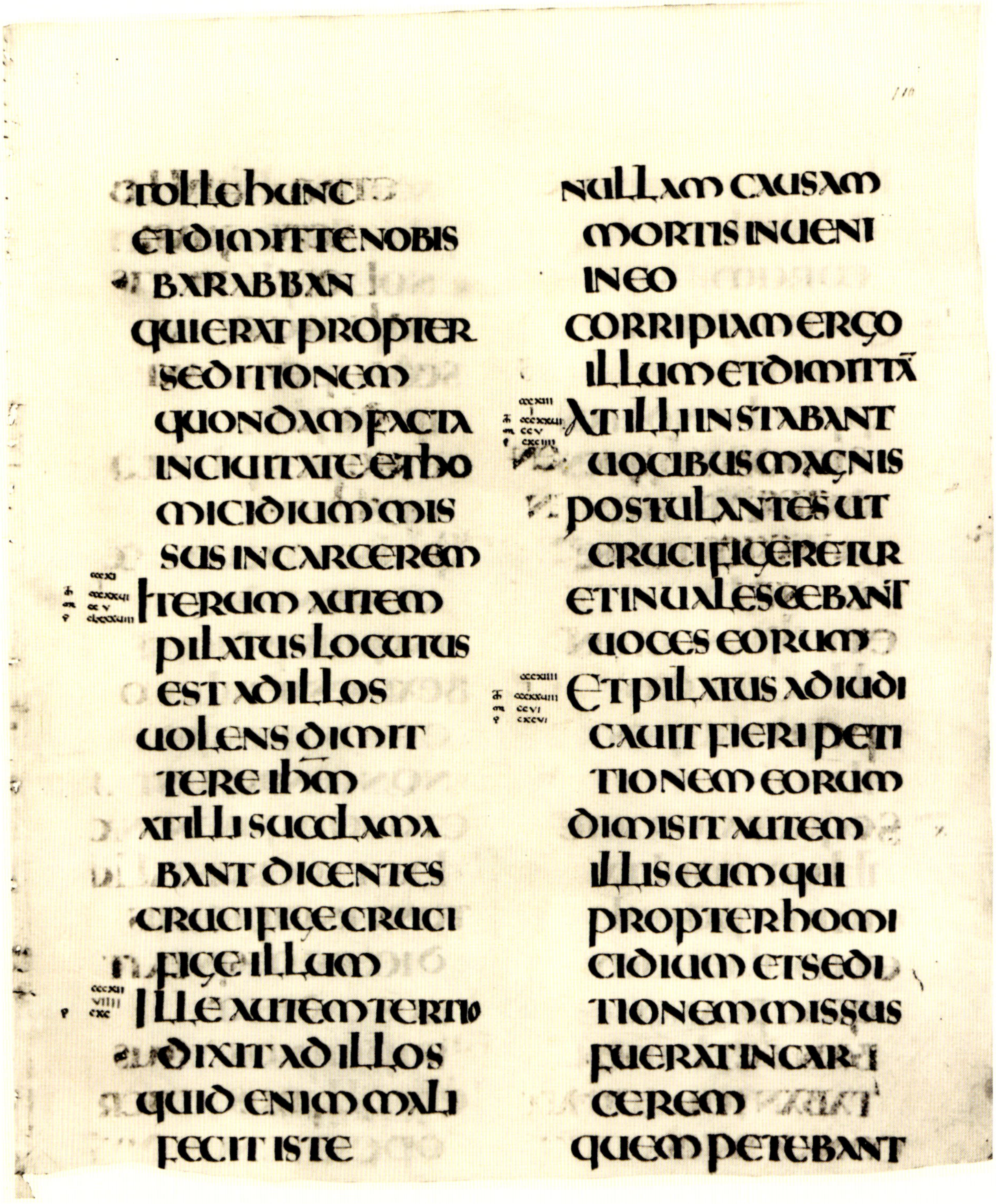
tolle hunc
et dimitte nobis
barabban
qui erat propter
seditionem
quondam facta
in ciuitate et ho
micidium mis
sus in carcerem
iterum autem
pilatus locutus
est ad illos
uolens dimit
tere ihm
at illi succlama
bant dicentes
crucifige cruci
fige illum
ille autem tertio
dixit ad illos
quid enim mali
fecit iste
nullam causam
mortis inueni
in eo
corripiam ergo
illum et dimittam
at illi instabant
uocibus magnis
postulantes ut
crucifigeretur
et inualescebant
uoces eorum
et pilatus adiudi
cauit fieri peti
tionem eorum
dimisit autem
illis eum qui
propter homi
cidium et sedi
tionem missus
fuerat in car
cerem
quem petebant

Fig. 5

4. The Stonyhurst Gospel, or The Cuthbert Gospel of John

Manuscript: English Province of the Society of Jesus, British Library, Loan 74.
Produced ca. 698 (690–716) at Wearmouth-Jarrow.
Parchment; 94 leaves; 13.5 x 9 cm.
Script: Uncial.
Facsimile on display: *The Stonyhurst Gospel of Saint John*. Ed. T. Julian Brown. Oxford: Roxburghe Club, 1969.

SEVERAL FEATURES of the Stonyhurst Gospel make it a fascinating example of an early gospel book. First of all, the manuscript is an incredibly small 13.5 x 9 cm., making it an early example of a portable extract from the Bible, and one of the smallest surviving manuscripts from Anglo-Saxon England. The manuscript is also significant for its binding (the "single most important bookbinding" of the period), which is the earliest western example (i.e., the earliest to survive in all of Europe) of the use of "Coptic" or unsupported sewing, "with red leather over wooden boards, moulded over a classical plant-scroll motif and tooled with interlace infilled in blue and yellow" (Brown 429). Further, a twelfth-century inscription notes that the gospel book was found in the coffin of St. Cuthbert (d. 687) when his remains were translated in 1104 (the manuscript could have been inserted when his body was first translated in 698). Marked readings in the text itself suggest that the manuscript was used in the mass of the dead, perhaps that for Cuthbert himself.

The opening on display, iii verso and f. 1r, shows the twelfth-century note about the discovery of the manuscript in the coffin of St. Cuthbert ("euangelium Iohannis quod inuentum fuerat ad capud beati patris nostri Cuthberti in sepulcro iacens anno translationis ipsius") and the opening of the gospel of John 1:1 ("In principio erat uerbum"). The facsimile is at the same size as the original. ✲

Brown, Michelle P. "Stonyhurst Gospel of St John." *The Blackwell Encyclopaedia of Anglo-Saxon England*. Ed. Michael Lapidge, John Blair, Simon Keynes, and Donald Scragg. Oxford, and Malden, MA: Blackwell, 1999. 429.

5. The Lindisfarne Gospels

Manuscript: London, British Library, MS Cotton Nero D.iv.

Produced ca. 698 in Northumbria, probably at Lindisfarne, and perhaps in association with the first translation of St. Cuthbert's body in 698.

Parchment; 258 leaves; 34 x 24 cm.

Decorated throughout.

Script: Insular half-uncial.

Principal contents:

Gospels of Matthew, Mark, Luke, and John, including prefatory material.

Facsimile on display: *Euangeliorum quattuor codex Lindisfarnensis.* Ed. T.D. Kendrick, et al. Zurich: Urs Graf Verlag, 1956.

OF NOTE IN THIS MANUSCRIPT are the interlinear translation and the colophon, both the work of a certain Aldred, provost of the community of St. Cuthbert at Chester-le-Street, and completed in 970. Though Bede was rumoured to have been working on a translation of the gospel of John from Latin into Old English at the time of his death, Aldred's interlinear translation (completed, as he reports it, with the help of God and St. Cuthbert) is the oldest surviving version of any part of the gospels in English. Aldred also adds a colophon which sketches (from tradition?) a production team for the manuscript, including an artist/scribe (Eadfrith, bishop of Lindisfarne, 698–721), a binder (Ædiluald, prior of Melrose), and a maker of the metalwork fittings or shrine (Bilfrith the anchorite). Michelle Brown notes that "the volume assimilates varied cultural influences: its 'Italo-Northumbrian' text exhibits Neapolitan liturgical features; its elegant 'reformed' Insular half-uncial script reflects the influence of Roman uncials; its evangelist portraits are indebted to Italo-Byzantine painting, interpreted in stylized form; its carpet pages betray possible Coptic influence; its canon tables, decorated incipit pages and initials apply the status-laden repertoires of Celtic and Germanic ornament to the new medium of the book" (288).

The openings on display show the cross-carpet page introducing St. Jerome's letter to Pope Damasus and the opening of that letter (ff. 2v–3r), as well as, in black and white, the colophon of Aldred which describes the men involved in the making of the manuscript (Backhouse 13). ✻

Backhouse, Janet. *The Lindisfarne Gospels.* Oxford: Phaidon Press, 1981.

Brown, Michelle P. "Lindisfarne Gospels." *The Blackwell Encyclopaedia of Anglo-Saxon England.* Ed. Michael Lapidge, John Blair, Simon Keynes, and Donald Scragg. Oxford, and Malden, MA: Blackwell, 1999. 288–89.

6. The St. Petersburg Bede

(FORMERLY KNOWN AS THE LENINGRAD BEDE)

Manuscript: St. Petersburg, National Library of Russia, MS Q.v.I.18.

Produced in Northumbria, probably at Wearmouth-Jarrow, within a few years of Bede's death in 735 (ca. 746?).

Parchment; 162 leaves; 27 x 19 cm.

Decorated; historiated initials (enlarged letters which contain pictures) at the beginning of each book; this manuscript is one of the earliest to include historiated initials.

Script: Anglo-Saxon minuscule.

Principal contents:

Bede. *Historia ecclesiastica gentis Anglorum* (*The Ecclesiastical History of the English People*).

Facsimile on display: *The Leningrad Bede: An Eighth-Century Manuscript of the Venerable Bede's "Historia ecclesiastica gentis Anglorum" in the Public Library, Leningrad*. Ed. Olof Arngart. Early English Manuscripts in Facsimile 2. Copenhagen: Rosenkilde and Bagger, 1952.

BEDE'S *Historia ecclesiastica gentis Anglorum*, usually known in English as *The Ecclesiastical History of the English People*, is our most important source for the early history of England. Completed in 731, the work begins with a description of the island and the arrival of Gaius Julius Caesar and the Romans (55–54 BCE) and takes the history to the year of the completion of the book. The St. Petersburg Bede is one of the earliest of some 130 manuscripts of Bede's history, which circulated exclusively in Latin until it was translated into Old English during the reign of King Alfred (871–99).

Though of tremendous importance for its Latin text of Bede, the manuscript also contains what may be the earliest written exemplar of English literature: *Cædmon's Hymn*. Arguably the most significant story in Bede's work is the account of the cowherd Cædmon, who, when pressed to sing at the evening meal, departed to be with his animals rather than take a turn. One particular evening, an angel appeared to him as he slept and commanded him to sing. Cædmon, insisting that it was impossible, nevertheless sang a glorious song of *frumsceaft* (first creation), which so impressed the residents of the monastery in which he worked that he was afterward regularly fed scripture in translation that he might ruminate upon it and bring forth exquisite verse in Old English. The story of this "miracle" is clearly important in the adoption of the vernacular as a medium for Christian theology, but Bede himself does not include Cædmon's words in his Latin history. Instead, Bede offers a Latin paraphrase and leaves it to later scribes and readers to add the Old English in the margins or at the end of the text. The grand tradition of English literature, therefore, begins as little more than an addition in the margins (a gloss, if you will) to a text in Latin.

The opening on display is f. 107a, which shows the text of *Cædmon's Hymn*, in Old English, at the bottom of the folio. ✻

7. The Moore Bede

Manuscript: Cambridge, University Library, MS Kk.5.16.
Probably produced in Northumbria, traditionally ca. 737, though perhaps slightly later.
Parchment; 128 leaves; 29.3 x 21.5 cm.
Script: Anglo-Saxon minuscule (though much of f. 128v is Caroline minuscule).
Principal contents:

Bede. *Historia ecclesiastica gentis Anglorum* (*The Ecclesiastical History of the English People*).

Facsimile on display: *The Moore Bede: An Eighth-Century Manuscript of the Venerable Bede's "Historia ecclesiastica gentis Anglorum" in Cambridge University Library (Kk. 5. 16)*. Ed. Peter Hunter Blair and Roger A.B. Mynors. Early English Manuscripts in Facsimile 9. Copenhagen: Rosenkilde and Bagger, 1959.

THE MOORE BEDE, so named after its early owner, Bishop John Moore (1646–1714), is another very early example of Bede's *Ecclesiastical History* in Latin. The manuscript is of interest partly because it was very likely at Aachen in 800 (perhaps sent from York, and perhaps at the request of Alcuin). However, it also contains the Old English version of *Cædmon's Hymn*, this time as an addition at the end of the entire history rather than as a marginal gloss beside Bede's Latin paraphrase.

The opening on display shows f. 128v, which includes the Old English version of *Cædmon's Hymn* (at the top of the folio, beginning "Nuscylun hergean hefaen ricaes uard metudæs maecti end his modgidanc") and several other additions in Caroline minuscule. ✻

8. The Codex Aureus

Manuscript: Stockholm, Kungliga Biblioteket, MS A.135.
Produced around the middle of the 8th century, probably at Canterbury.
Parchment; 193 leaves; 39.5 x 31.4 cm.
Decorated throughout.
Script: Uncial.
Principal contents:
Gospels of Matthew, Mark, Luke, and John, including prefatory material.
Facsimile on display: *The Codex Aureus: An Eighth-Century Gospel Book: Stockholm, Kungliga Bibliotek, A.135*. Ed. Richard Gameson. 2 vols. Early English Manuscripts in Facsimile 28–29. Copenhagen: Rosenkilde and Bagger, 2001-2002.

THE EDITOR of the facsimile of the *Codex Aureus*, Richard Gameson, calls it "the most opulent surviving medieval English manuscript" (1: 11). The manuscript contains alternating purple and white pages, and employs different-coloured inks on the alternate pages. On the white pages, one may see black, brown, and orange ink; on the purple, gold, silver, white, and orange. Artistically, the style is a mixture of insular forms and continental ones. Of particular interest is the later history of the manuscript, which was apparently seized by Vikings and held for ransom.

The openings on display show a portion near the beginning of Matthew (f. 10v) and a Chi-rho monogram plus embellished *autem*, a page in decorative display capitals, with a ninth-century Old English note describing the seizure and ransom of the manuscript (f. 11r), and the portrait of John and the opening of his gospel (ff. 150v–151r). The letter detailing how the book was ransomed from a "heathen army" by a certain Aelfred, his wife, Werburg, and their daughter Alhthryth reads as follows:

> *In the name of our Lord Jesus Christ.* I, Earl Alfred, and my wife Werburg procured this book from the heathen invading army with our own money; the purchase was made with pure gold. And we did that for the love of God and for the benefit of our souls,

and because neither of us wanted these holy works to remain any longer in heathen hands. And now we wish to present them to Christ Church to God's praise and glory and honour, and as thanksgiving for his sufferings, and for the use of the religious community which glorifies God daily in Christ Church, in order that they should be read aloud every month for Alfred and for Werburg and for Alhthryth, for the eternal salvation of their souls, as long as God decrees that Christianity should survive in that place. And also I, Earl Alfred, and Werburg beg and entreat in the name of Almighty God and of all his saints that no man should be so presumptuous as to give away or remove these holy works from Christ Church as long as Christianity survives there. ✲

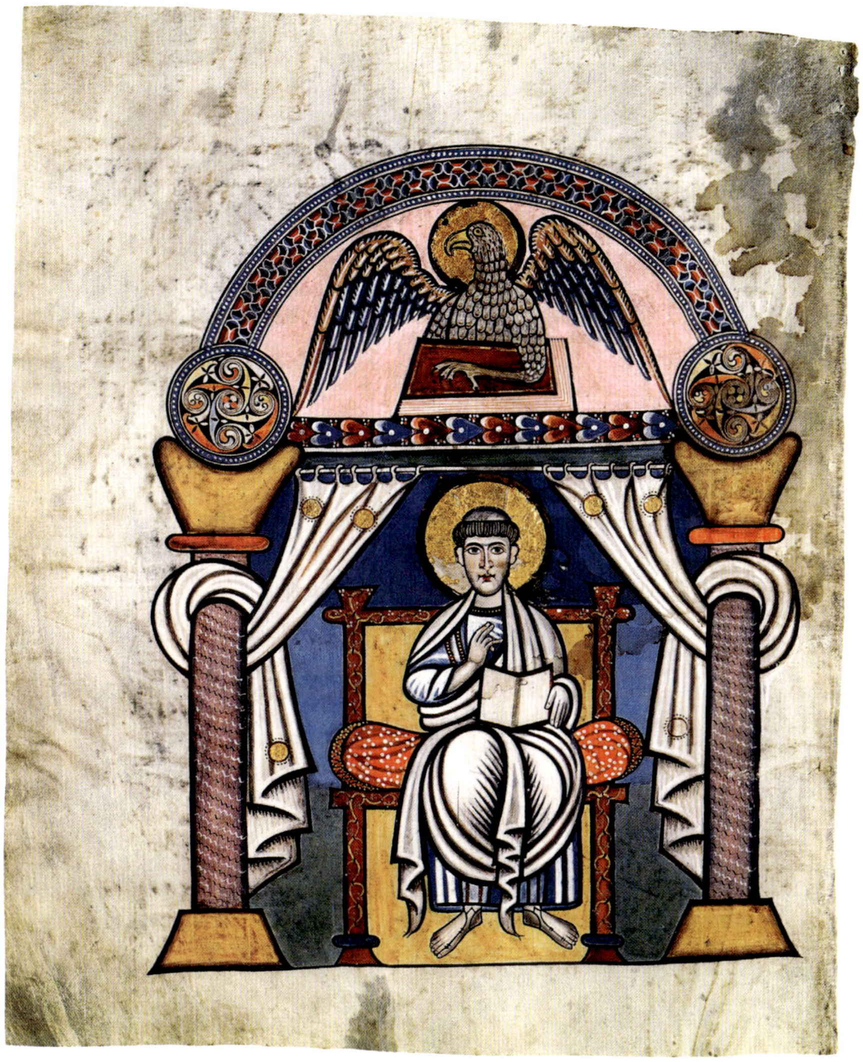

Fig. 6

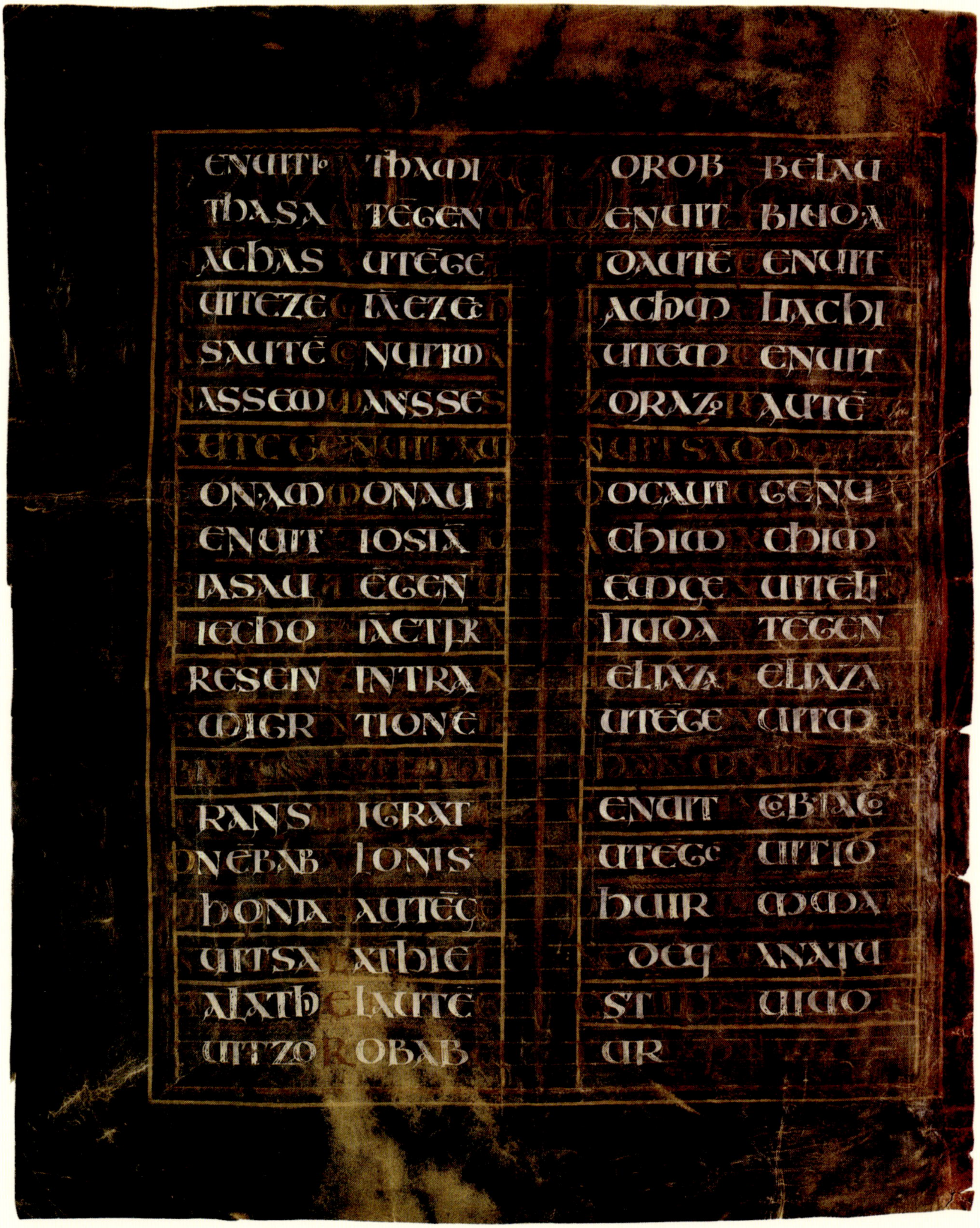

Fig. 7

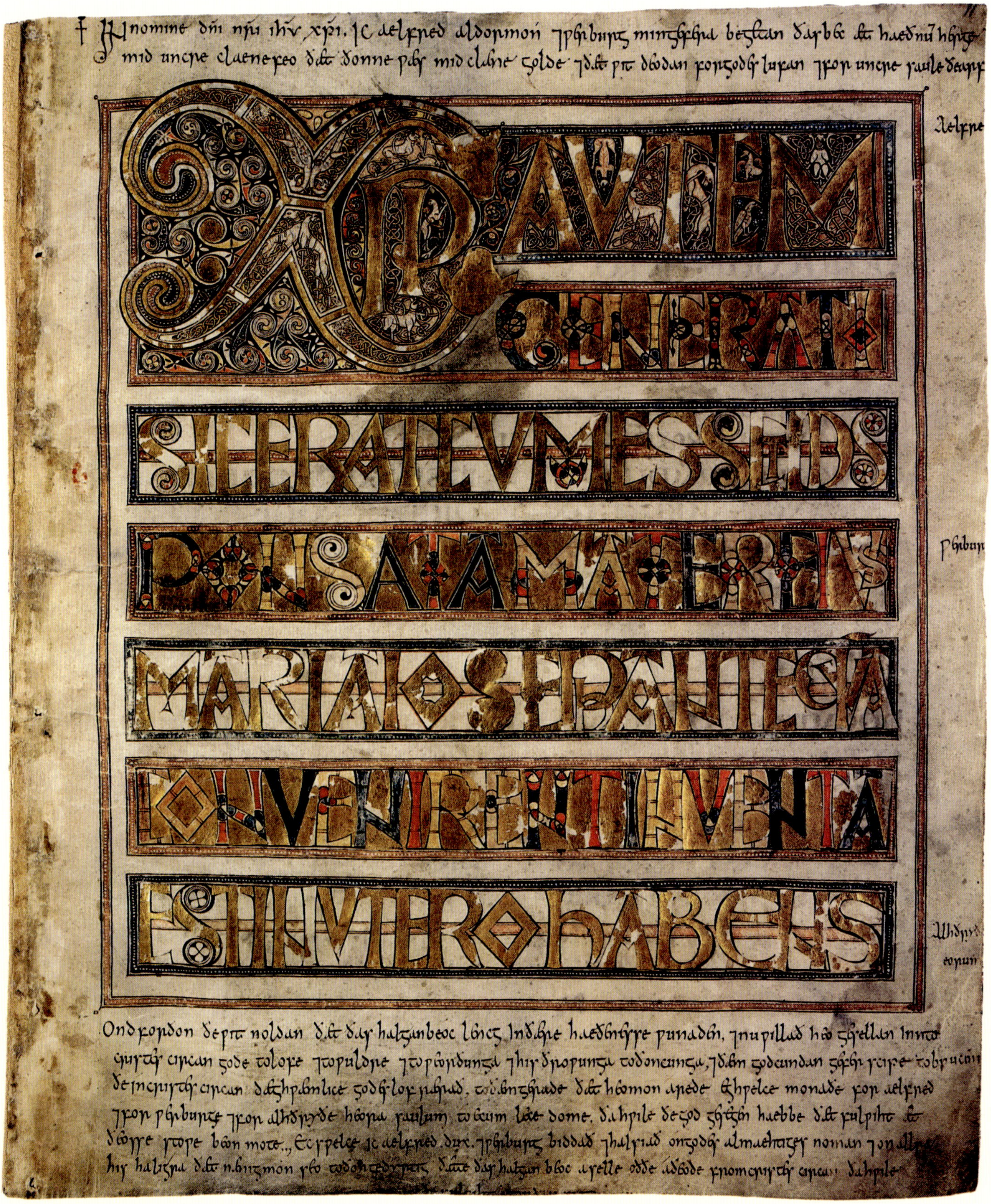

9. The Book of Kells

Manuscript: Dublin, Trinity College Library, MS A.1.6 (58).
Produced in the 8th or 9th centuries (ca. 800?), in the British Isles, perhaps at Iona.
Fine vellum; 340 leaves; 33 x 25 cm.
Decorated throughout.
Script: Insular (or sometimes Irish) majuscule.
Principal contents:
Gospels of Matthew, Mark, Luke, and John (though John ends at John 17:13 and the rest is missing), including prefatory material.
Facsimile on display: *The Book of Kells: MS 58, Trinity College Library Dublin*. Ed. Peter Fox. Lucerne: Faksimile Verlag, 1990.

VERY LITTLE is known for certain about the origin of *The Book of Kells*. The manuscript gets its name from the Abbey of Kells in Kells, County Meath in Ireland, where it was kept for much of the medieval period. Though the Abbey of Kells was founded around 800, it is unlikely to have seen the production of the manuscript. *The Book of Kells* was for a long time thought to have been made during the lifetime of St. Columba, who founded the monastery of Iona in 563. However, analysis of the manuscript has proven that this cannot be the case. Still, the most likely scenario is that the manuscript was created at Iona, in the late eighth or early ninth century, and then removed to the Abbey of Kells by monks fleeing the raids of the Vikings, who had famously sacked Lindisfarne, for example, in 793. Some scholars have even argued that the book was created at Lindisfarne, and then moved to Iona before ending up in Kells.

The Book of Kells was certainly at Kells in the twelfth century, as some of its blank pages were used to record land charters of the abbey at that date. There is also an entry in the *Annals of Ulster* for 1006 which suggests that a certain "Gospel of Columkille" [Columba] was stolen and stripped of its decorative cover before being found buried several months later; this may or may not refer to *The Book of Kells* itself.

The first opening on display, f. 34r, is known as the Chi-rho page, after the first two letters in the abbreviated Greek form of the name of Christ. The Chi-rho page of the *Book of Kells* is one of the most widely known images from a medieval manuscript. The three letters form the main part of the image, and two other Latin words are visible: *autem* ('now') and *generatio* ('birth'). The second image is f. 290v which prefaces the gospel of John and shows the symbols of the four evangelists. ✻

Farr, Carol Ann. *The Book of Kells: Its Function and Audience.* British Library Studies in Medieval Culture 4. London: British Library; Toronto: University of Toronto Press, 1997.

Lewis, Susanne. "Sacred Calligraphy: The Chi Rho Page in the Book of Kells." *Traditio* 36 (1980): 139–59.

Pulliam, Heather. *Word and Image in the Book of Kells.* Dublin: Four Courts Press, 2006.

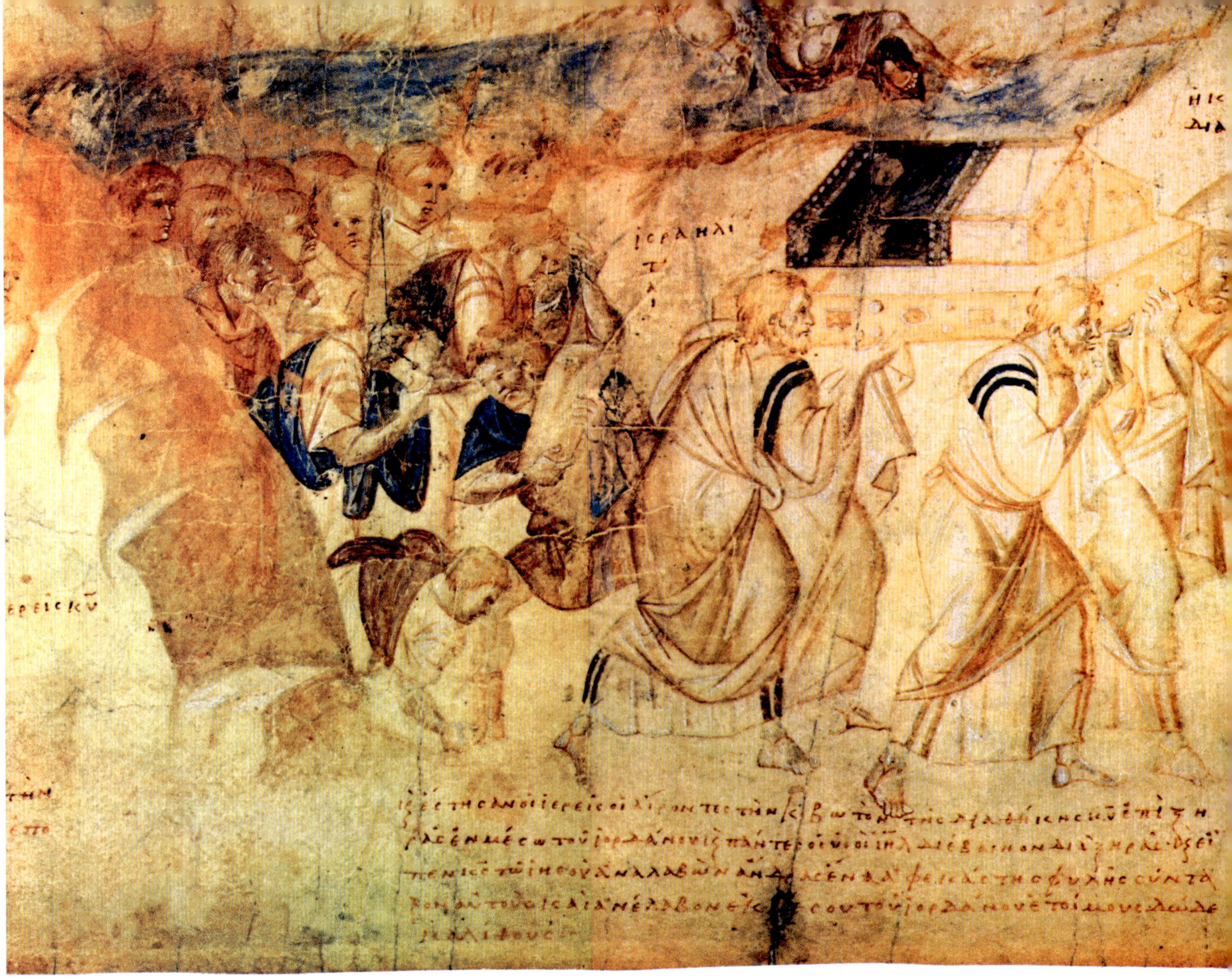

Fig. 8

10. The Joshua-Roll

Manuscript: Vatican City, Biblioteca Apostolica Vaticana, Cod. Pal. graec. 431.

Produced in the 10th century, probably in Constantinople.

Parchment; roll; 31 x 10 m.

Decorated throughout.

Script: Greek majuscule and minuscule forms.

Principal contents:

Joshua 1–12, in Greek (the Septuagint version), abbreviated.

Facsimile on display: *Josua-Rolle: Codex Vaticanus Pal. graec. 431*. (Scroll and commentary volume.) Ed. Otto Mazal. Codices e Vaticanis selecti 43; Codices selecti phototypice impressi 77-77*. Graz: Akademische Druck- u. Verlagsanstalt, 1983–1984.

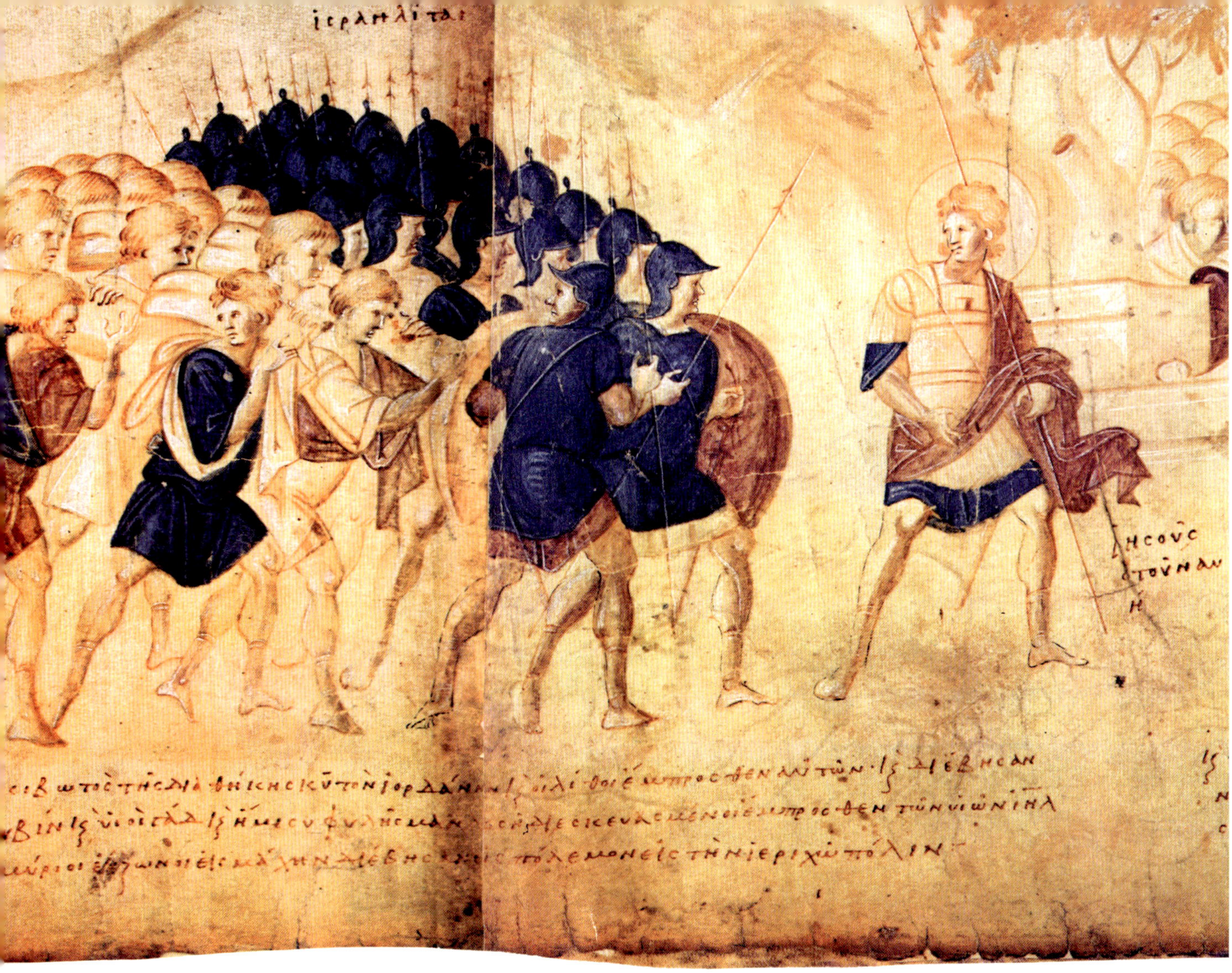

A REVIEWER of Kurt Weitzmann's book on the *The Joshua-Roll* called the roll "one of the most important and difficult problems of Byzantine art" (Katzenellenbogen 421). Most scholars are generally agreed about the text of the roll, which is clearly a tenth-century Greek version of the Old Testament book of Joshua, but the images are difficult, and a broad range of opinion has been put forward as to their dates and origin. The illustrations are in the form of a continuous frieze, though the artist was probably working from an exemplar with individual pictures and may have been deliberately reviving "the continuous frieze form of the two triumphal columns in Constantinople" (Katzenellenbogen 423). It has also been suggested that the roll, especially on account of the odd slanting of the images, was intended as a model for a column (i.e., images wrapped around the column), but this theory has not been generally accepted. The style of painting is known as grisaille (shades of grey).

The opening on display shows Scene 5 and Scene 6, depicting the crossing of the Jordan (Joshua 3:17 and 4:1–3 and 8) and the resumption of the march of the Israelites after crossing the Jordan (Joshua 4:11–13). ✲

Katzenellenbogen, Adolf. "Kurt, Weitzmann: *The Joshua Roll: A Work of the Macedonian Renaissance*." *Speculum* 26 (1951): 421-25.

Weitzmann, Kurt. *The Joshua Roll: A Work of the Macedonian Renaissance*. Studies in Manuscript Illumination 3. Princeton: Princeton University Press, 1948.

11. The Nowell Codex
(ALSO KNOWN AS THE *Beowulf* MANUSCRIPT)

Manuscript: London, British Library, MS Cotton Vitellius A.xv.
Produced ca. 1000 in England.
Parchment; 206 leaves; 19.5 x 11.5–13 cm.
Illustrated; twenty-nine miniatures in *The Wonders of the East.*
Script: Insular minuscule (two distinct styles, however, divided at *Beowulf*, l. 1939 [f. 172v, l. 3] in the word *scyran*).
Principal contents:
1) Ff. 94r–98r: *The Passion of St. Christopher* (incomplete at beginning).
2) Ff. 98v–106v: *The Wonders [or Marvels] of the East.*
3) Ff. 107r–131v: *The Letter of Alexander to Aristotle.*
4) Ff. 132r–201v: *Beowulf.*
5) Ff. 202r–209v: *Judith* (incomplete at beginning and end).
Facsimile on display: *The Nowell Codex: British Museum, Cotton Vitellius A.xv, Second MS.* Ed. Kemp Malone. Early English Manuscripts in Facsimile 12. Copenhagen: Rosenkilde and Bagger, 1963.

COTTON VITELLIUS A.XV is a composite manuscript, consisting of two separate codices, now known as the Southwick Codex and the Nowell Codex. The former is written in a twelfth-century hand and contains our only extant copy of King Alfred's Old English version of Augustine's *Soliloquies*. The latter, perhaps most famous for containing *Beowulf*, is usually dated to around the year 1000, and is named after an inscription identifying Laurence Nowell (1510/20?–1571?) as the owner. When these two codices were joined is unknown, but it may have been during their ownership by Sir Robert Bruce Cotton (1571–1631), and thus not a medieval development at all. The codex contains five texts (listed above): three prose texts and two poetic texts, one illustrated and four not, two missing portions at the beginning or the end, and every single one suffering the damage from the disastrous Cotton Library fire of 1731. In other words, *Beowulf* survived just barely, in somewhat odd company, and in several places damaged beyond our ability certainly to reconstruct the text. The most convincing argument, however, for the collection of the manuscript as a whole is that it was assembled by someone with an interest in monsters, for monsters and monstrous behaviour seem key elements in each of the five texts which the codex preserves.

The opening on display shows the beginning of *Beowulf*, one of the longest (3182 lines) surviving Old English poems and certainly the most important:

Hwæt! We gardena   in geardagum
þeodcyninga   þrym gefrunon
hu ða æþelingas   ellen fremedon. (1–3)

[Listen! We of spear-Danes in days of old
of people-kings the glory have heard
how those nobles deeds of courage
performed.]

Over the word *egsode* (line 5), one can see that someone has written the word "feared." This was probably Laurence Nowell himself, attempting a gloss to the text. ✲

Orchard, Andy. *Pride and Prodigies: Studies in the Monsters of the "Beowulf"-Manuscript*. Cambridge: D.S. Brewer, 1995.

Facsimile on display: *Electronic Beowulf* 2.0. Book with CD-ROM (2 disks). Ed. Kevin S. Kiernan. London: British Library, 2004.

"This is a reissue of an innovative 2-disk CD-ROM which is a complete colour facsimile of the Beowulf poem, one of the British Library's earliest and most famous manuscripts. Uniquely, it also includes fibre optic and ultra-violet readings of damaged and erased text" (publisher's description).

12. An Anglo-Saxon Scientific Miscellany

Manuscript: London, British Library, MS Cotton Tiberius B.v.

Produced in the second quarter of the 11th century at Winchester(?).

Parchment; 147 leaves; 26 x 21.8 cm.

Illustrated; principal items (calendar, *Aratea*, *Wonders*) are illustrated in colour.

Script: generally Caroline minuscule (Latin) and Anglo-Saxon minuscule (Old English)

Principal contents:

1) Ff. 2–19: calendar, computus matters, tables.
2) Ff. 32v–49v: Cicero, *Aratea*.
3) Ff. 78v–87v, *The Wonders [or Marvels] of the East.*

Facsimile on display: *An Eleventh-Century Anglo-Saxon Illustrated Miscellany: British Library Cotton Tiberius B. V part I, together with leaves from British Library Cotton Nero D. II.* Ed. Patrick McGurk, et al. Early English Manuscripts in Facsimile 21. Copenhagen: Rosenkilde and Bagger, 1983.

PATRICK MCGURK, the principal editor of the facsimile, calls this manuscript "one of the most lavishly illustrated secular manuscripts to survive from the early Middle Ages" (15). The illustrations appear in the three principal works in the manuscript, including a series of seasonal illustrations in the calendar, 27 drawings to accompany Cicero's Latin translation of the Greek astronomical poem *Aratea*, and 38 framed drawings, one for each section of the text of *The Wonders of the East*. The manuscript also includes the earliest medieval *mappa mundi* (f. 56v). The miscellany is probably best known for its bilingual text (Latin and Old English) of *The Wonders of the East*, which is closely related to that in London, British Library, MS Cotton Vitellius A.xv (Item 11). The illustrations, on the other hand, seem to come from a different tradition, and are certainly more polished than those in the *Beowulf*-manuscript. There is a third English manuscript of *Wonders* as well, the twelfth-century Oxford, Bodleian Library, MS Bodley 614.

The opening on display, ff. 81v–82r, shows a section from *The Wonders of the East* (images for entries 12–15 and text for entries 13–16). The order of the entries is Latin text first, Old English translation, then picture, so the pictures do not correspond to the text below. The four images on the two leaves depict men with manes like lions who are twenty feet tall, have mouths as big as fans and sweat blood; the race known as Hostes, definitely cannibals; the wild animals known as Lertices, with donkey's ears and sheep's wool and

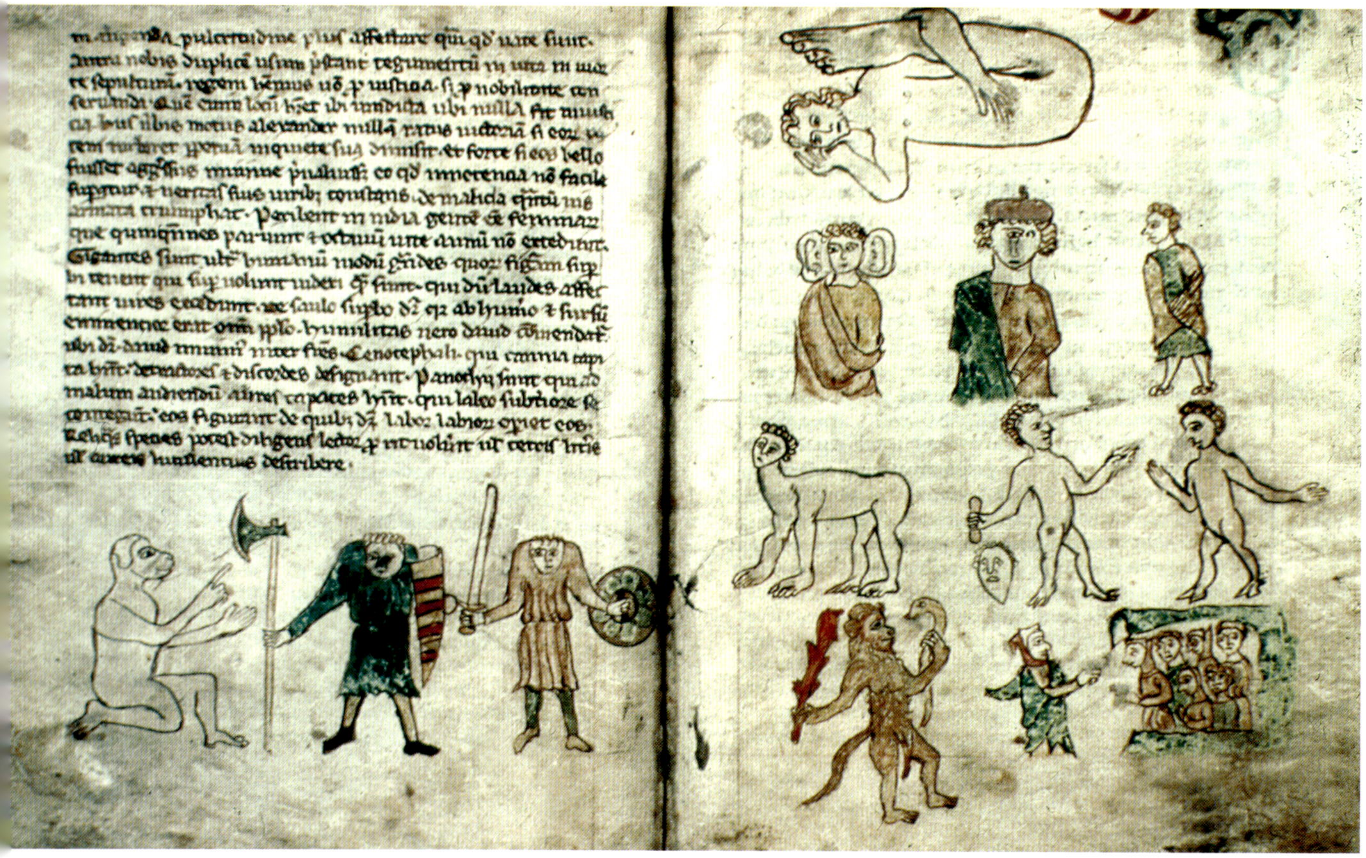

Fig. 9

bird's feet; and square men (eight feet by eight feet!) without heads but who have their eyes and mouths in their chests, known as Blemmyae.

Item 12B: The accompanying photograph shows an opening from a thirteenth-century bestiary (Oxford, Bodleian Library MS Douce 88 Pt. 2, ff. 69v–70r), with a chart of the "monstrous races" described in Pliny's *Natural History*. In the lower left we see a dog-headed man (Cynocephalus), said to live in the mountains of India; next there are two Blemmyae, men with faces on their chests, who live in the deserts of Libya (according to Pliny) — they are also mentioned by Shakespeare. On the right-hand page, from the top: a Sciapod (shadow-foot), who is one-legged but extremely swift (so rarely seen), and who spends much of the day sheltering from the hot sun beneath the shadow of his foot. Row 2: a Panotius ("all-ears") — this race is said to be very shy and, when approached, a Panotius flaps his ears and flies away (they also use their ears for blankets when the temperature drops); next is a Cyclops, with one eye in the middle of the head: Homer placed them in Sicily, but other writers place them in India; next is what appears to be a dog-footed man. Row 3: an Artibatira, one who walks on all-fours, described by Pliny; a horned man or a Straw-drinker (the latter being men who grow a natural straw on their faces and breathe and drink [but they cannot eat] through it); a goat-footed man (satyr). Row 4: a lion-man, and a group of what may be Speechless Men, a race of men who can communicate only with gestures. ✻

13. The Domesday Book

Produced in 1086–1087 for William I of England ("William the Conqueror").
Parchment; 413 pages (Great Domesday) and 475 pages (Little Domesday).
Decorated; rubrication of county titles and corrections.
Principal contents:
Domesday: a record of towns and villages under the control of William I.
Facsimile on display: *Great Domesday* and *Little Domesday Book*. 12 vols. with 12 cases of unbound quires. London: Alecto Historical Editions, 1986–2000.

The Domesday Book is effectively a survey or census (mainly for the purposes of taxation) of all of England. In fact, it consists of two separate works, *Great Domesday* and *Little Domesday*. The former contains records for most of England in a condensed form, while the latter covers Essex, Norfolk, and Suffolk, which were not part of *Great Domesday*. The survey was undertaken at the behest of King William I, who, after long consultation with his council, desired to know everything about the land which he had conquered. The entry for 1085 in MS E of the *Anglo-Saxon Chronicle* describes the process:

> Then he sent his men all over England into every shire to ascertain how many hundreds of "hides" of land there were in each shire, and how much land and live-stock the king himself owned in the country, and what annual dues were lawfully his from each shire.... So very thoroughly did he have the inquiry carried out that there was not a single "hide," not one virgate of land, not even — it is shameful to record it, but it did not seem shameful to him to do — not even one ox, nor one cow, nor one pig which escaped notice in his survey.

The opening on display, f. 2v, shows part of the record for Kent and Canterbury. ✻

Hallam, Elizabeth M. *Domesday Book through Nine Centuries*. London and New York: Thames and Hudson, 1986.
Maitland, F.W. *Domesday Book and Beyond: Three Essays in the Early History of England*. Cambridge: Cambridge University Press, 1897.
Wood, Michael. *The Doomsday Quest: In Search of the Roots of England*. London: BBC Books, 2005.

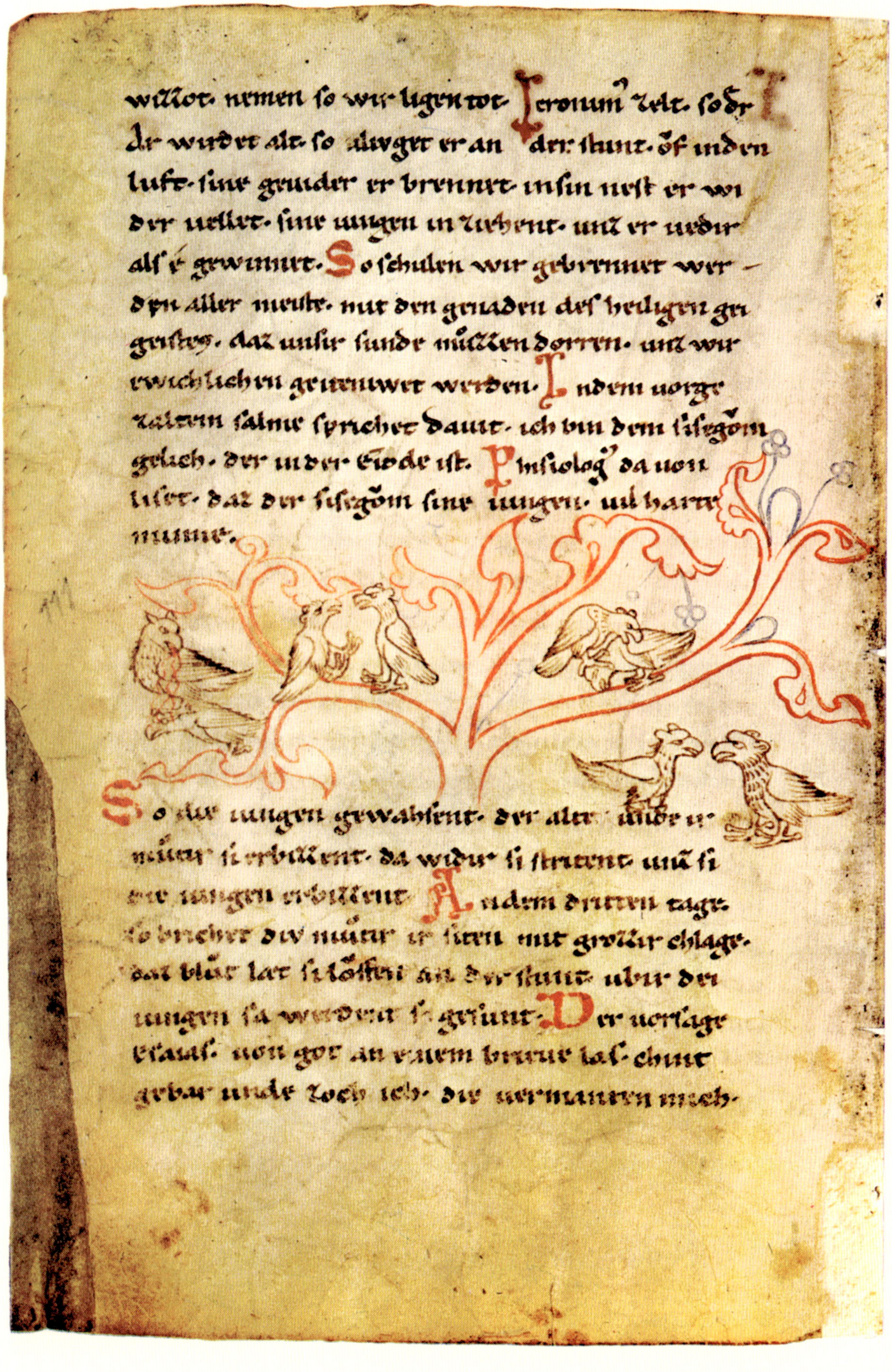
willot. nivwen so wir ligen tot. Jeronimus zelt. so der
adr wirdet alt. so fluget er an der sunne. vf in den
luft. sine gevider er brennet. in sin nest er wi
der vellet. sine iungen in zuchent. und er uedir
als er gewinnet. So schulen wir gebrennet wer-
den aller meiste. mit den genaden des heiligen ge
gistes. daz unsir sunde muzzen dorren. und wir
ewichlichen geniuwet werden. In dem vorge
zalten salme sprichet dauit. ich bin dem sisegom
gelich. der in der einode ist. Phisiologus da von
liset. daz der sisegom sine iungen vil harte
minne.
So die iungen gewahsent. der alte vnde div
muter si erbilgent. da wider si strichent vnd si
die iungen erbiltent. An dem dritten tage.
so brichet div muter ir siten mit grozzer chlage.
daz bluot lat si fliezen an der stunt. ubir den
iungen sa werdent si gesunt. Der wissage
ysaias. von got an einem brieue las. chint
gebar unde zoch ich. die vermanten mich.

Fig. 10

14. The Millstätter Genesis and Physiologus

Manuscript: Klagenfurt, Kärnter Landesarchiv, Cod. 6/19.
Produced in South Bavaria (Carinthia) in the first half of the 12th century.
Parchment; 167 leaves; 20 x 13 cm.
Illustrated throughout.
Principal contents:
Genesis, Exodus, Physiologus.
Facsimile on display: *Millstätter Genesis und Physiologus Handschrift: vollständige Facsimile-ausgabe der Sammelhandschrift 6/19 des Geschichtsvereines für Kärnten im Kärntner Landesarchiv, Klagenfurt*. Ed. Alfred Kracher. Codices selecti phototypice impressi 10. Graz: Akademische Druck- u. Verlagsanstalt, 1967.

KÄRNTER LANDESARCHIV 6/19 is an early twelfth-century manuscript written in Middle High German which contains an unusual selection of texts. The manuscript begins with illustrated cycles from Genesis and Exodus which are of great interest in themselves, but also includes an illustrated physiologus, also known as a bestiary, a collection of short observations and moralizing about the animals of the world (for a fuller explanation of such texts, see Item 18). This is the earliest German manuscript to contain extensive and lavish illustrations.

The opening on display, f. 97v, shows an image of the pelican (from the physiologus): the young pelicans fight with the old, and an effort is made to revive a dead youngster with blood. It is commonly reported in the physiologus that, after three days, the pelican reanimates her young with her blood, just as Christ returned mankind to life after three days in the tomb. ✲

15. The Anglo-Catalan Psalter

Manuscript: Paris, Bibliothèque nationale de France, Ms. latin 8846.
Produced in Canterbury (1180–1190) and Catalonia (1330–1340).
Parchment; 178 leaves; 48.0 x 33.2 cm.
Decorated and illuminated; 28 historiated initials; more than 140 miniatures.
Script: Early Gothic bookhand.
Facsimile on display: *Psalterium glosatum / Salterio Anglo-Catalán*. 2 vols. Barcelona: M. Moleiro Editor, 2004-2006.

THIS MANUSCRIPT is rather curious in having been completed in two different places at two different periods. Work on it seems to have begun in late twelfth-century Canterbury, in a style reminiscent of another twelfth-century manuscript from Canterbury, the Eadwine Psalter (Cambridge, Trinity College Library, MS R.17.1). Then, sometime in the thirteenth century, the manuscript found its way to Catalonia, where, in the early fourteenth century, additional work was done upon it, including a series of new miniatures by Ferrer Bassa and other Catalan miniaturists. Some decades later the manuscript appears in France, and it may have been owned by Jean duc de Berry (a number of other books from his collection are also included in this exhibition). In the late eighteenth century the manuscript was given to Napoleon Bonaparte, and thus became part of his Bibliothèque impériale, which later became the Bibliothèque nationale.

In this Psalter the Psalms are presented in Latin in three versions ("Hebrew," "Roman," and "Gallican"). The "Gallican" version is given prominence by the amount of space reserved for it, as well as the fact that it is provided with interlinear and marginal glosses. Although the text is Latin, there are small fragments of Anglo-French and Old English on several pages.

The opening on display is from the beginning of the manuscript; on the left page is the conclusion of St. Jerome's preface to the Psalms; on the right we see the opening lines of Psalm 1. The top half of f. 5v is taken up with a large miniature in four frames, offering a Christian reading of this Psalm: 1) in the upper left we see Christ, with two attendant angels, pointing to the Book of the Law (cf. Ps. 1:2, "his will is in the law of the Lord"); 2) then, beneath images of the sun and moon (offering a cosmic context), we see Christ pulling a man by his cloak away from the right-hand frame (the "chair of pestilence") towards the left (the Book of the Law); 3) the "cathedra pestilentie" ("chair of pestilence") of verse 1, upon which sits a king holding a sword, before whom appear those who seek audience and bring gifts, but behind him is a devil prodding him with a torch; 4) below is a large scene, showing a river, being the "running waters" of verse 3 (the righteous man is said to flourish like a tree planted by running waters); on the left is the river spirit creating the river by pouring it from a vessel; in the centre is an upturned face blowing (a wind spirit, causing dust to blow; cf. v. 4 which says that the wicked are like dust driven by the wind); on the right is a group of wicked men (in the forefront is the same king who appears above) being speared by devils and dragged into the flames of hell (cf. vv. 5–6). On the facing page, f. 6r, we see three large decorated letters "B," representing the beginning of the first word "Beatus" in each of the three versions of the first verse; the third "B" is accompanied by the rest of the letters of the opening phrase "Beatus vir"; above each "B" is a man with a book, representing the "Beatus vir," the "blessed man," holding the Book of the Law. ✲

16. The Heidelberg *Rolandslied*

Manuscript: Heidelberg, Universitätsbibliothek, Cod. Pal. germ. 112.
Produced possibly in the region of Regensburg or Hessen-Thüringen, late 12th c.
Parchment; 123 leaves; 21.0 x 15.0 cm.
Decorated; large rubricated initial letters; 39 line drawings (a few with traces of colour).
Script: Early Gothic minuscule.
Facsimile on display: *Das Rolandslied des Pfaffen Konrad: Einführung zum Faksimile des Codex Palatinus Germanicus 112 der Universitätsbibliothek Heidelberg*. Ed. Wilfried Werner and Heinz Zirnbauer. 2 vols. Facsimilia Heidelbergensia 1. Wiesbaden: Dr. Ludwig Reichert Verlag, 1970.

THE *Chanson de Roland*, composed around 1100, is a medieval French epic that tells of how Roland, one of the twelve champions with whom the Emperor Charlemagne surrounded himself, was killed in an ambush in the Pass of Roncesvalles. The story is based upon a historical incident that occurred when Charlemagne crossed the Pyrenees on 15 August 778. According to the *Chanson*, the ambush and Roland's death were arranged by Roland's personal enemy, Ganelon, whose treachery became a byword in medieval Europe: Ganelon and Judas Iscariot are mentioned together, for instance, in Chaucer's "Nun's Priest's Tale." The *Chanson*, then, is the story of the death through treachery of a great hero, and of the terrible vengeance that Charlemagne took upon Ganelon. This manuscript is of a German version of the story, produced perhaps a century after the composition of the French original.

The opening on display, ff. 57v–58r, includes an illustration showing a tower under siege. The missing corner of the page is of interest; given the cost of parchment, even imperfect sheets were fully utilized. Note also the visible "pricking" down the side of the page: preparing a leaf for writing included poking a series of equidistant pin pricks (through several pages at once) along both vertical edges to indicate the points where the bottoms of the lines of writing should be set, so that the scribe could achieve the appearance of equally spaced and straight lines.

The entire manuscript has been reproduced online, and can be examined on the website of the Universitätsbibliothek Heidelberg at <http://digi.ub.uni-heidelberg.de/cpg112>. ✻

17. The Donaueschingen *Nibelungenlied*

Manuscript: Karlsruhe, Badische Landesbibliothek, Cod. Donaueschingen 63.
Produced in the Voralberg region of the Tyrol, ca. 1225.
Parchment; 114 leaves; 24.5 x 16.5 cm.
Decoration: a few elaborated initials, some light rubrication.
Script: Caroline minuscule.
Facsimile on display: *Das Nibelungenlied: Manuscript C from the Fürstenberg Court Library, Donaueschingen*. Ed. Heinz Engels. 2 vols. [Oxford]: Phaidon Press, 1968.

THE *Nibelungenlied*, one of the most important works of medieval German literature, is the folk-epic of Siegfried, his death, and the vengeance, enacted by his widow, which caused the destruction of two great nations. The manuscript also contains the *Nibelungenklage*, something of a supplement, probably by another author, which offers a series of laments for those who fell in the *Nibelungenlied*. The tales told here were the basis for many later literary works as well as Wagnerian operas. The *Nibelungenlied* was composed ca. 1200, the *Klage* soon thereafter, and this manuscript is the earliest known manuscript of either; nevertheless, it is not usually used as the base text for modern editions, since the text is considered to be of a "second recension," a "revised" version of the story.

The manuscript is not illustrated, but there are several decorated initial letters, one of which is seen here in the additional photograph, reproduced from the Badische Landesbibliothek website. The opening of the facsimile on display, ff. 59v–60r, shows some of the text, written in a clear Caroline minuscule. Since parchment was very expensive to produce, scribes used even defective leaves, and here a cut in the parchment has been repaired with stitching.

The entire manuscript has been reproduced online, and can be examined on the Badische Landesbibliothek website: <http://www.blb-karlsruhe.de/blb/blbhtml/nib/einfuehrung-obhof.html>. ✻

Obhof, Ute. *Die "Nibelungenlied"-Handschrift C: Codex Donaueschingen 63*. Joseph Freiherr von Laßberg (1770–1855) und seine Bibliothek 2. Karlsruhe: Kulturstiftung der Länder, in association with the Badische Landesbibliothek, 2005.

18. The Bodley Bestiary

Manuscript: Oxford, Bodleian Library, MS Bodley 764.
Produced in England between 1220 and 1250.
Vellum: 137 leaves; 29.8 x 19.5 cm.
Decorated and illustrated throughout.
Script: Gothic bookhand ("black letter"; "littera textualis formata"), though not on display here.
Facsimile on display: *Bestiary, being an English Version of the Bodleian Library, Oxford M.S. Bodley 764, with All the Original Miniatures Reproduced in Facsimile*. Trans. and ed. Richard Barber. London: Folio Society, 1992.

THE PHYSIOLOGUS (a term which simply means "writer about nature" or "student of nature") or bestiary as it is also known, has its probable origins in Greek, in second- or third-century Alexandria. The earliest examples usually begin with a biblical quotation about an animal, discuss the physical characteristics and habits of the animal, and then offer some moral or religious interpretation of the animal and how it can be observed and understood as a lesson for mankind. As Richard Barber puts it, "each creature is therefore a kind of moral entity, bearing a message for the human reader" (7). These works were translated into many languages (for example, Armenian, Syriac, and Ethiopic), but the Latin tradition, which it seems must begin by the fourth century, is most significant for later medieval versions. By the time of Bodley 764, the physiologus had grown to embrace many other medieval texts as sources, most significantly, Isidore of Seville's great *Etymologiae* (*Etymologies*), but also later texts and authors such as Gerald of Wales, Hugh of Fouilloy, and Peter of Cornwall. The richly illustrated versions seem to have been largely an English development, especially popular in the first half of the thirteenth century. Though no complete physiologus survives from Anglo-Saxon England, the Exeter Book, a famous anthology of Old English poetry (Exeter, Cathedral Library, 3501), includes three entries in verse: the panther, the whale, and the partridge.

The opening on display, pp. 68–69, shows the "eale" ("yale") and the wolf, with Barber's translation of the entries. ✻

Badke, David. "The Medieval Bestiary: Animals in the Middle Ages." <http://bestiary.ca/>.

The Bestiary: Being a Reproduction in Full of the Manuscript. Ii.4.26 in the University Library, Cambridge, With Supplementary Plates from Other Manuscripts of English Origin, and a Preliminary Study of the Latin Bestiary as Current in England. Ed. M.R. James. Oxford: Roxburghe Club, 1928.

19. The Munich *Tristan und Isolde*

Manuscript: Munich, Bayerische Staatsbibliothek, Cgm. 51.

Produced probably in Schwabia or Bodensee, ca. 1240–1250.

Parchment; 110 leaves; ca. 23.5 x 16.5 cm.

Decoration: 15 miniatures.

Script: Protogothic book script.

Facsimile on display: *Tristan und Isolde, mit der Fortsetzung Ulrichs von Türheim: Faksimile-Ausgabe des Cgm 51 der Bayerischen Staatsbibliothek München*. 2 vols. Stuttgart: Müller und Schindler, 1979.

GOTTFRIED'S *Tristan und Isolde* is one of the great medieval romances and, with the *Nibelungenlied* and Wolfram's *Parzival*, one of the masterpieces of medieval German literature. The work was composed in the early years of the thirteenth century but was left incomplete at Gottfried's death (traditionally 1210); this manuscript includes the continuation of the work by Ulrich von Türheim (ca. 1235), and the manuscript seems to have been produced soon thereafter.

Tristan, a knight in the court of King Mark of Cornwall, travels to Ireland to free Cornwall from paying tribute to Gurman, King of Ireland; Tristan succeeds by killing Gurman's brother, the giant Morold, and eventually returns to Cornwall with the praise of Isolde, Gurman's daughter, on his lips. King Mark then tells Tristan to journey again to Ireland and to win Isolde's hand for Mark, so Tristan embarks, disguised as "Tantris." He finds that Gurman's kingdom is being ravaged by a dragon, and the king has offered Isolde's hand to whichever hero can free the kingdom. The three illustrations exhibited show how Tantris succeeds in killing the dragon (top panel of f. 67r; the dragon is labelled "Serphant") and cuts out its tongue; however, the fumes from the dragon's mouth render him unconscious, at which point the queen's steward arrives, pretends to battle the dead dragon (middle panel), and then carries its body (bottom panel) back to court to claim Isolde's hand. Tantris, however, has the dragon's tongue, by which eventually he is proven to be the true dragon slayer. He is then truly in torment, however, for he must take Isolde to Cornwall to marry King Mark despite the fact that he is in love with her himself.

20. The Munich *Parzival*

Manuscript: Munich, Bayerische Staatsbibliothek, Cgm. 19.

Produced in Schwabia, ca. 1240–1250.

Parchment; 75 leaves; 30.0 x 21.0 cm.

Decorated initials (in red and blue); four pages of miniatures (ff. 49–50) to accompany *Parzival*.

Script: Protogothic book script.

Facsimile on display: *Parzival, Titurel, Tagelieder: Cgm 19 der Bayerischen Staatsbibliothek München; Transkription der Texte von Gerhard Augst, Otfried Ehrismann und Heinz Engels, mit einem Beitrag zur Geschichte der Handschrift von Fridolin Dressler*. 2 vols. Stuttgart: Müller und Schindler, 1970.

ANOTHER of the great German chivalric romances, *Parzival* is an expansion of Chrétien de Troyes' story of the Grail and its seeker (Sir Parsifal, not Galahad, was the first Grail Knight). The romance appears in this manuscript along with two other works by Wolfram, his *Titurel* (an elegy on a pair of unhappy lovers) and *Tagelieder* (a small collection of songs).

The facsimile is open at the fourth page of miniatures, divided into several scenes illustrating the latter stages of the story. The top panel shows a feast in the Grail Castle; there are banderoles not filled in, but which were intended to include the names of Parzival on the left, Amfortas, lord of the Grail Castle, in the middle, and, in the place of honour on Amfortas' right, the pagan knight, Feirefiz. The central panel illustrates an episode slightly earlier in the story, as Parzival meets his wife, Condwiramurs, and their two sons. The bottom panel shows two scenes that follow after the feast depicted in the top panel. The pagan Feirefiz, who has fallen in love with the Grail Maiden, is told that she might receive him, and he might see the Grail, if he is baptized, to which he immediately consents; his baptism is seen here on the left; on the right, Feirefiz is granted a vision of the Grail, and his pagan idol is destroyed. ✲

21. The Northumberland Bestiary

Manuscript: Los Angeles, J. Paul Getty Museum, MS 100 (formerly Alnwick, Alnwick Castle Library, MS 447).

Produced in England, ca. 1250.

Parchment; 75 leaves; 21.6 x 17.1 cm.

Illustrated; 112 illustrations.

Facsimile on display: *A Thirteenth-Century Bestiary in the Library of Alnwick Castle*. Ed. Eric George Millar. Oxford: Roxburghe Club, 1958.

THE Northumberland Bestiary is another example of a thirteenth-century English bestiary in Latin, and is closely related to British Library, Royal 12 C.xix (from the end of the twelfth century). The bestiary is no longer in the library at Alnwick Castle: it was sold in 1990 to an unknown buyer for $5.85 million. After being inaccessible for the last sixteen years, the bestiary was purchased in 2007 by the J. Paul Getty Museum of Los Angeles, so that it is now once again available to the scholarly community.

The opening on display, ff. 46v–47r, shows the *serra*, a large winged fish with a proclivity for racing ships (f. 46v) and the *aspido delone*, or the whale (f. 47r), one of the most famous creatures of the medieval bestiary. The nature of the whale is such that unsuspecting sailors take it for an island and anchor there, only to be drowned when their activities cause the whale to submerge. Demons deceive in just such a way, tricking people until they can draw them down into hell. ❋

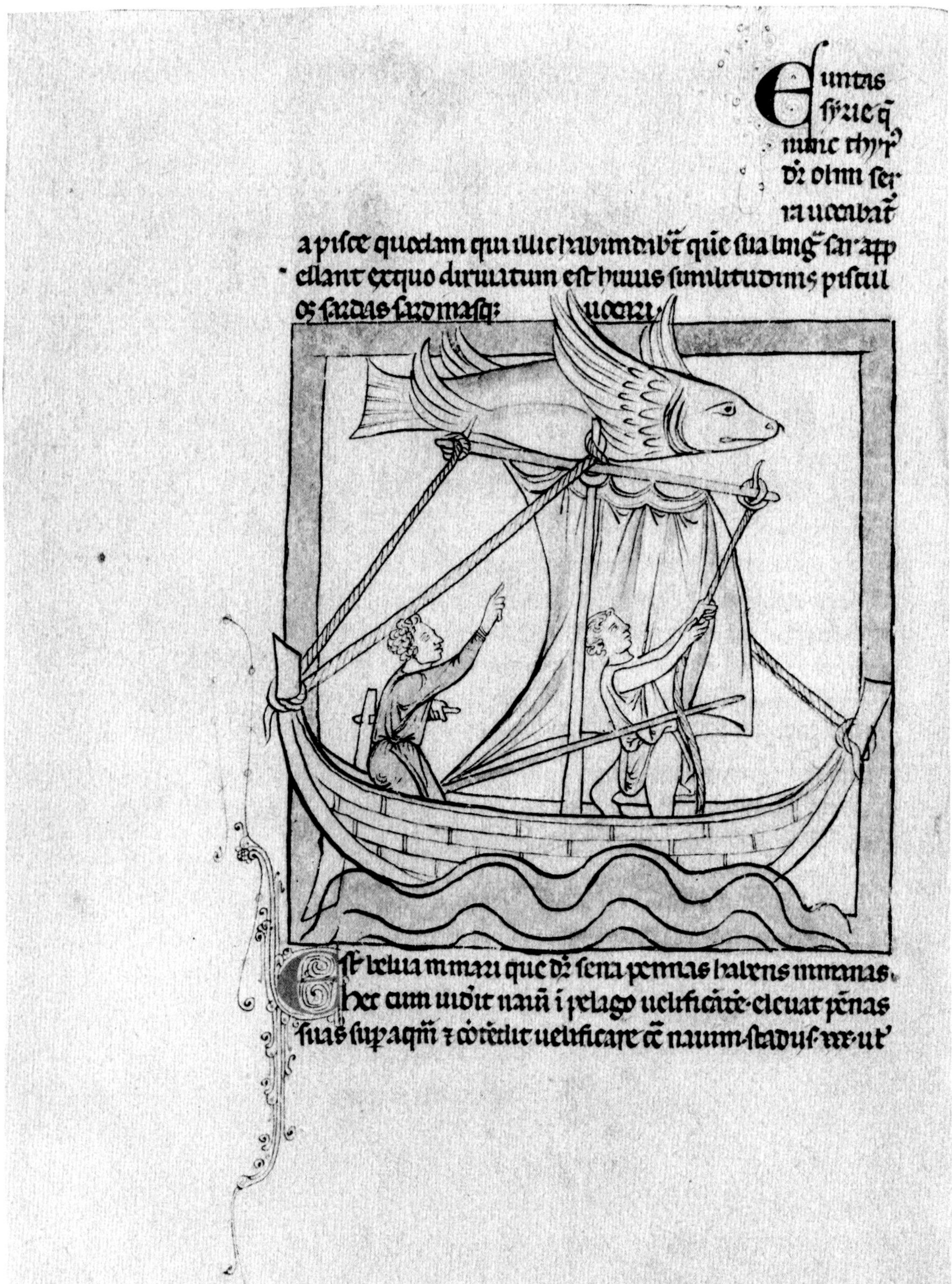

Fig. 11

xl. 7 nō sustinens laborem deficit 7 deponēs pēnas ad se att
rahit eas. Vñ uo maris iam lassam reportant ad locū suū in
pfundum. Hec belua figuram hƀt huius scli. Nauis uo itor
hƀt exēplum qui sine periculo 7 naufragio fidei transierūt
p medias huius mūdi pcellas 7 tempestas. Serra uero idest
belua illa que nō ualuit uelificare cū naui figuram illorum
gerit qui in inicio ceperūt bōis opib; insistere. postea nō per
manētes ī eis uicti sunt diuisis in cōrū genib; que illos tamq̄
fluctuantes maris ūn mgūt us: ad inferos. nō eni incipien
tib; s; pseuantib; premium promittitur.

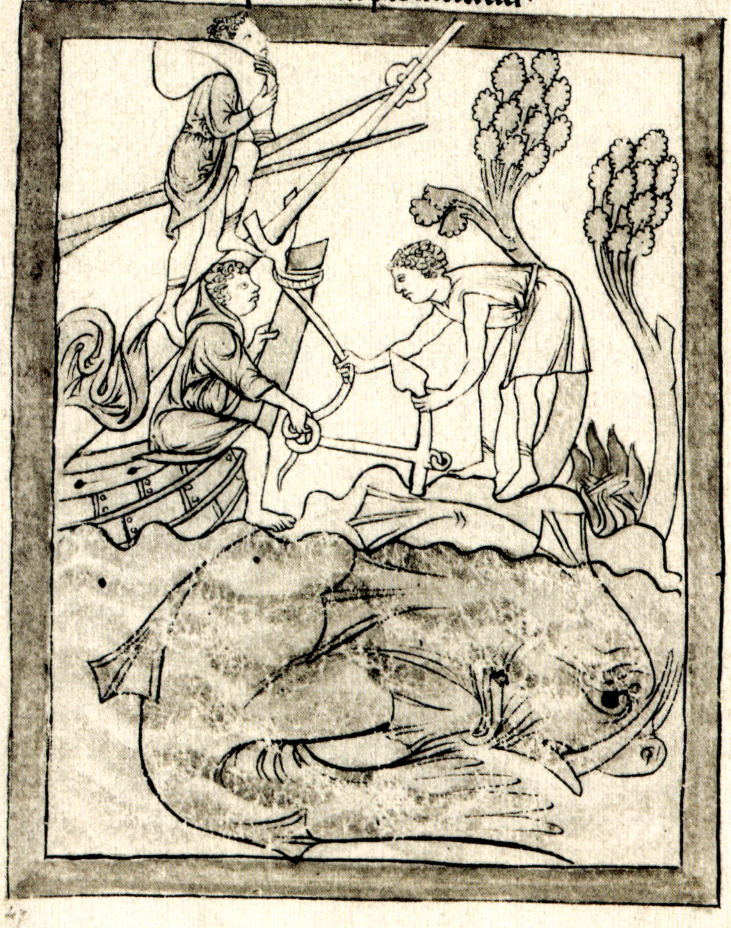

22. The Trinity College Apocalypse

Manuscript: Cambridge, Trinity College Library, MS R.16.2.
Produced in Northern France or Southern England (perhaps St. Alban's Abbey?), ca. 1250.
Fine vellum; 32 + 3 leaves; 43 x 30.5 cm.
Decorated and illustrated throughout.
Principal contents:
The Apocalypse, or Revelation of John, in Anglo-Norman French.
Facsimile on display: *The Trinity College Apocalypse*. Ed. Peter H. Brieger. 2 vols. London: Eugrammia Press, 1967.

WHILE BESTIARIES were enormously popular in England between 1200 and 1400, so were illustrated manuscripts of the final book of the New Testament, the Apocalypse or Revelation of John. In the Trinity College Apocalypse, we have what Janet Backhouse has called "the most sumptuous of all the thirteenth-century apocalypses" (35).

The opening on display, ff. 14v–15r, shows scenes and text from Rev. 13:1–15. The first image on f. 14v depicts the dragon transferring power to the beast from the sea, which in turn makes war on the saints. On f. 15r, the false prophet emerges from the earth and performs miracles; those who will not worship are executed, and others kneel before the image of the beast. ✻

Backhouse, Janet. "The Trinity College Apocalypse." *The Burlington Magazine* 111, no. 790 (1969): 35-6.

Die Trinity-Apokalypse / The Trinity Apocalypse: Cambridge, Trinity College Library, MS. R.16.2. Ed. David McKitterick. Lucerne: Faksimile Verlag, 2004.

The Trinity Apocalypse (Trinity College Cambridge, MS R.16.2). (Book plus CD-ROM.) Ed. David McKitterick. British Library Studies in Medieval Culture. London: British Library; Toronto: University of Toronto Press, 2005.

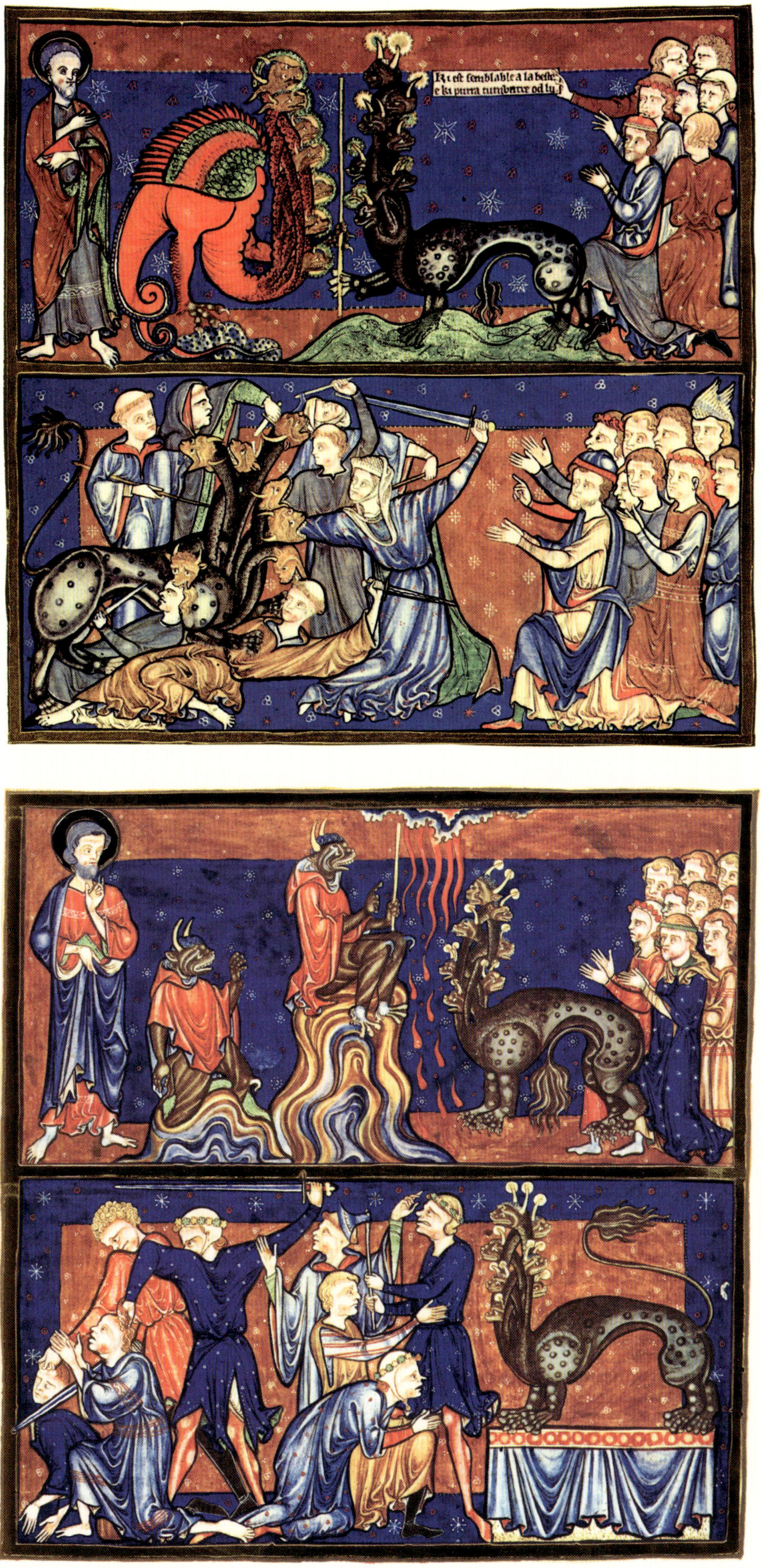

Fig. 12, 14v (above), 15r (below)

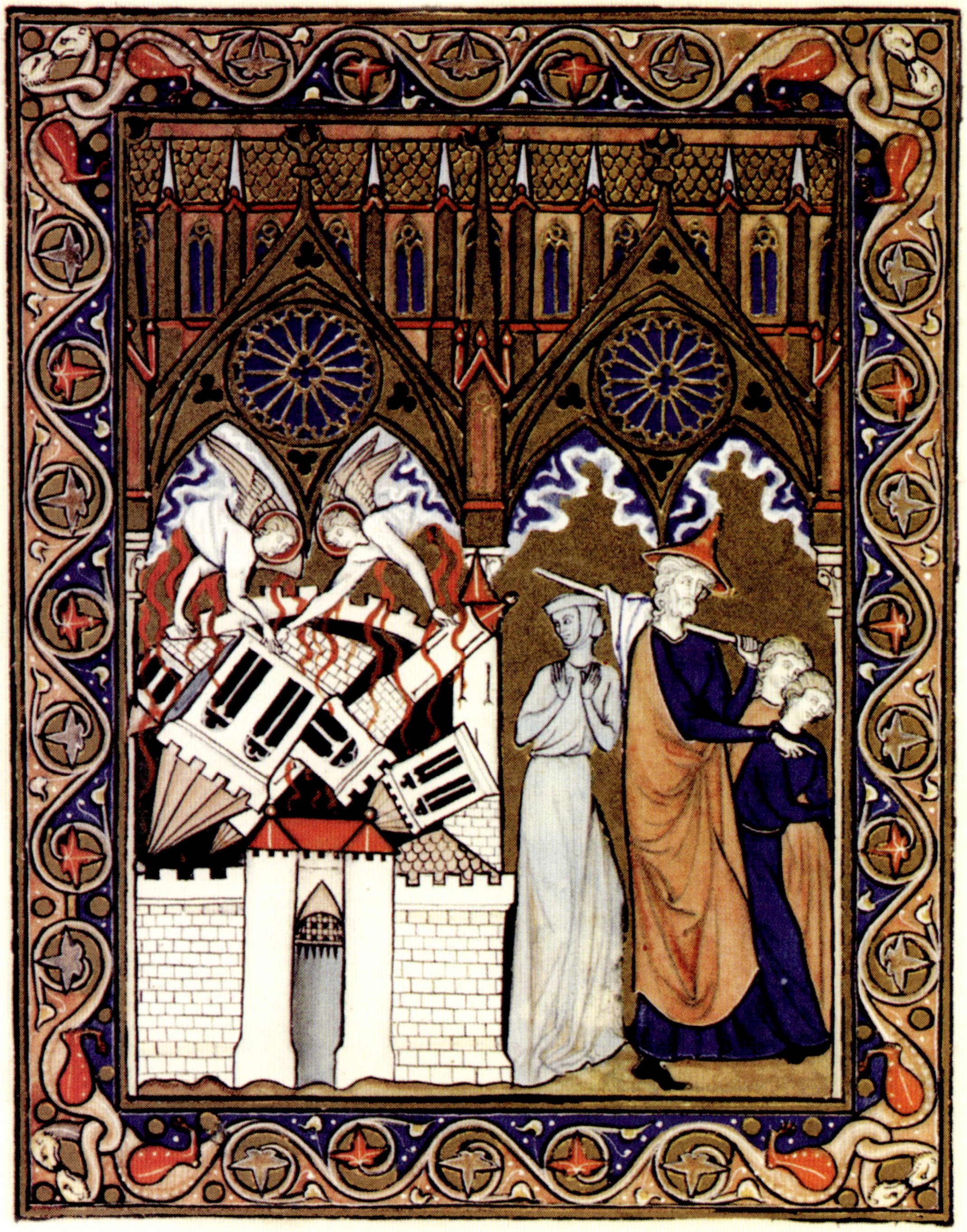

Fig. 13A (f. 9v)

23. The Psalter of St. Louis, King of France

Manuscript: Paris, Bibliothèque nationale de France, Ms. latin 10525.
Produced in Paris, between 1258 and 1270.
Parchment; 260 leaves; 21.0 x 14.5 cm.
Decorated and illuminated; coloured initials; 78 full-page miniatures (in a sequence preceding the text of the Psalter) and 7 partial-page miniatures within the Psalter.
Script: Protogothic book script, with capitals in alternating gold and blue.
Facsimile on display: *Le psautier de Saint Louis*. 2 vols. Codices selecti phototypice impressi 37. Graz: Akademische Druck- and Verlagsanstalt, 1972.

THIS is the personal Psalter of Louis IX of France (1236–1270), small and portable but lavishly decorated, and "personalized" with many images and heraldic symbols referring to the French nation and to the person of King Louis. There are, for instance, parallels between King Louis and King David, the Psalmist, represented in some of the images within the Psalter. Louis was himself later venerated as a saint, primarily by the French royal family; Item 28 in this exhibition, the Book of Hours of Jeanne d'Évreux (one of Louis' royal descendants), includes the Office of St. Louis as well as an image of Jeanne kneeling at his shrine.

The text of the Psalms is preceded by a set of 78 full-page miniatures, illustrating Old Testament stories, each set beneath an architectural canopy, and dominated by burnished gold-leaf backdrops. It is said that there is a close similarity between these miniatures and the design of stained glass windows in the Sainte Chapelle in Paris. Some 163 images related to this Psalter are reproduced in the Bibliothèque nationale's "Mandragore" image database, <http://mandragore.bnf.fr/>.

The opening on display is from the initial sequence of Old Testament miniatures. On f. 9v we see the destruction of the cities of Sodom and Gomorrah, whose citizens angered God with their iniquity. On f. 10r is the Sacrifice of Isaac by his father, Abraham. As the Bible tells the story, this event is a revelation of the fact that God does not wish the ritual killing of humans, but accepts animal sacrifices instead: thus an angel prevents Abraham from killing his son, and Abraham offers, in his son's place, a ram caught by the branches of a nearby bush. Christian exegetes also understood the story as offering a typological precursor of the crucifixion of Jesus, the sacrifice of the Son by his Father, and so the wrath of God illustrated in the panel on the left is here juxtaposed with an image, on the right, illustrating the mercy of God, in the foreshadowing of future Redemption by means of the sacrifice of God's Son. Note in both miniatures the golden "sky," which may signify to the viewer that such sacred events take place under the light of heaven. ✲

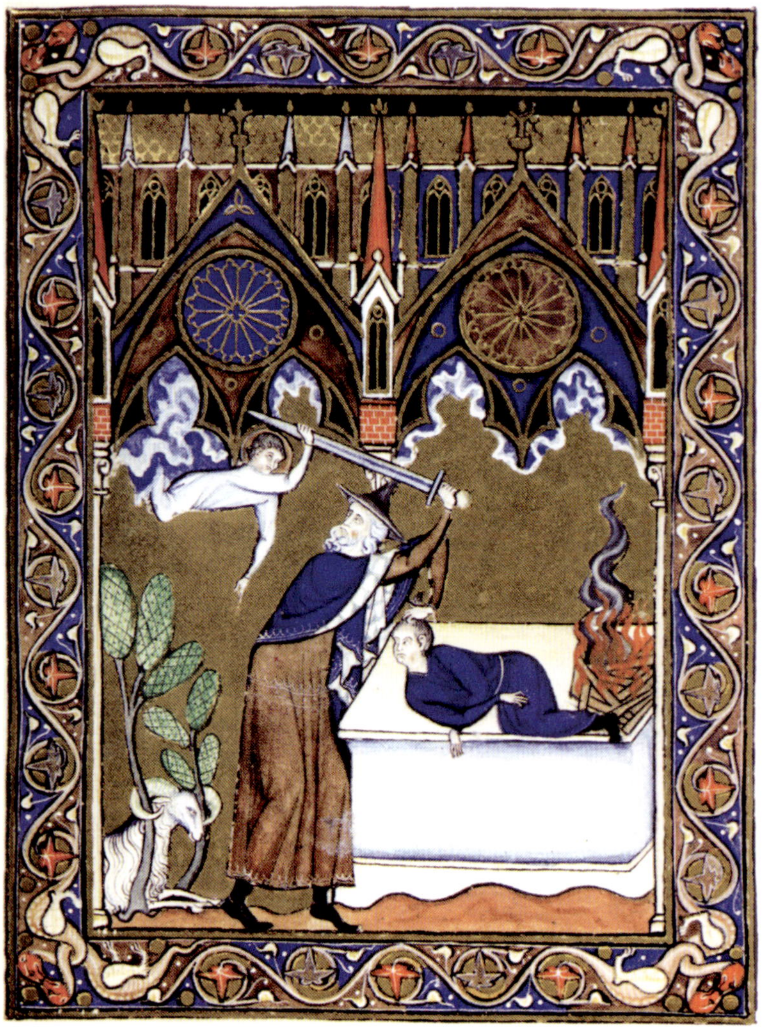

Fig. 13B (f. 10r)

24. The Hereford Map

Manuscript: Hereford, Hereford Cathedral Library.
Produced in Hereford by Richard of Haldingham, ca. 1300.
Parchment: 1.59 x 1.29–1.34 m.
Facsimile on display: *The World Map by Richard of Haldingham in Hereford Cathedral, circa AD 1285*. London: Royal Geographical Society, 1954.

THE HEREFORD MAP, as with many medieval maps, is not what we would generally call a map today. As Scott Westrem says, the Hereford Map is a "presentation of cosmological, ethnographical, geographical, historical, theological, and zoological information about the inhabited parts of the earth" (xv). The "map" is the largest and earliest document of its kind to survive from the medieval period, and includes over a thousand different inscriptions and more added illustrations. In essence, then, the "map" functions much more as an encyclopedia than as any kind of a navigational guide, and its information is culled from a range of classical, late antique, and medieval sources, including the Bible, Pliny, Solinus, Jerome, Martianus Capella, Orosius, Isidore, and Aethicus Ister.

The portion on display shows the section of the map which depicts England, squeezed into a corner and relatively insignificant compared to the Far East, which is fascinating for its images of monsters and marvels, many of which also appear in *The Wonders of the East* (Item 12). ✲

Harvey, P.D.A. *Mappa Mundi: The Hereford World Map*. London: British Museum, in association with Hereford Cathedral, 1996.

Westrem, Scott D. *The Hereford Map: A Transcription and Translation of the Legends with Commentary*. Turnhout: Brepols, 2001.

25. The Peterborough Bestiary

Manuscript: Cambridge, Corpus Christi College, MS 53.
Produced in England between 1304 and 1321.
Parchment; 105 + 1 leaves; 34.8 x 23.6 cm.
Decorated and illustrated: 104 miniatures; 108 decorated initials.
Principal contents:
Psalter; Chronicles of England and Peterborough Abbey; bestiary.
Facsimile on display: *A Peterborough Psalter and Bestiary of the Fourteenth Century*. Ed. Montague Rhodes James. Oxford: Roxburghe Club, 1921.

CORPUS CHRISTI COLLEGE MS 53 contains a somewhat unusual selection of texts. As the preface to the volume makes clear, Psalters were generally some of the most lavish productions of the early medieval period, at least until the Book of Hours takes over early in the fourteenth century. The Psalms of the Peterborough Psalter contain many illustrations and much ornamentation, but the manuscript as a whole is noteworthy not only for the Psalms and how they are presented, but also for the chronicles of England (Brutus to Edward I) and of Peterborough Abbey and, most unusually, an illustrated bestiary from f. 189. This particular bestiary organizes its contents into five sections, on beasts, birds, reptiles, serpents, and fish, though, by the last section, the illustrations are no longer a prominent part of the text.

The opening on display, f. 189r, shows the beginning of the bestiary, the first beast of which is *leo*, or the lion. Of especial interest is the miniature with five intersecting circles, including depiction of the lion, pursued by hunters, erasing his tracks with his tail, raising a cub, born dead, to life with a roar on the third day, gazing on a serpent, sniffing at a dead man, and, finally, eating a monkey, which Ambrose says will cure the lion of sickness. ✼

Das Bestiarum aus Peterborough / The Peterborough Bestiary: Cambridge, Corpus Christi College, Parker Library, MS 53 (fol. 189–210). Ed. Christopher de Hamel and Lucy Freeman Sandler. 3 vols. Lucerne: Faksimile Verlag, 2003.

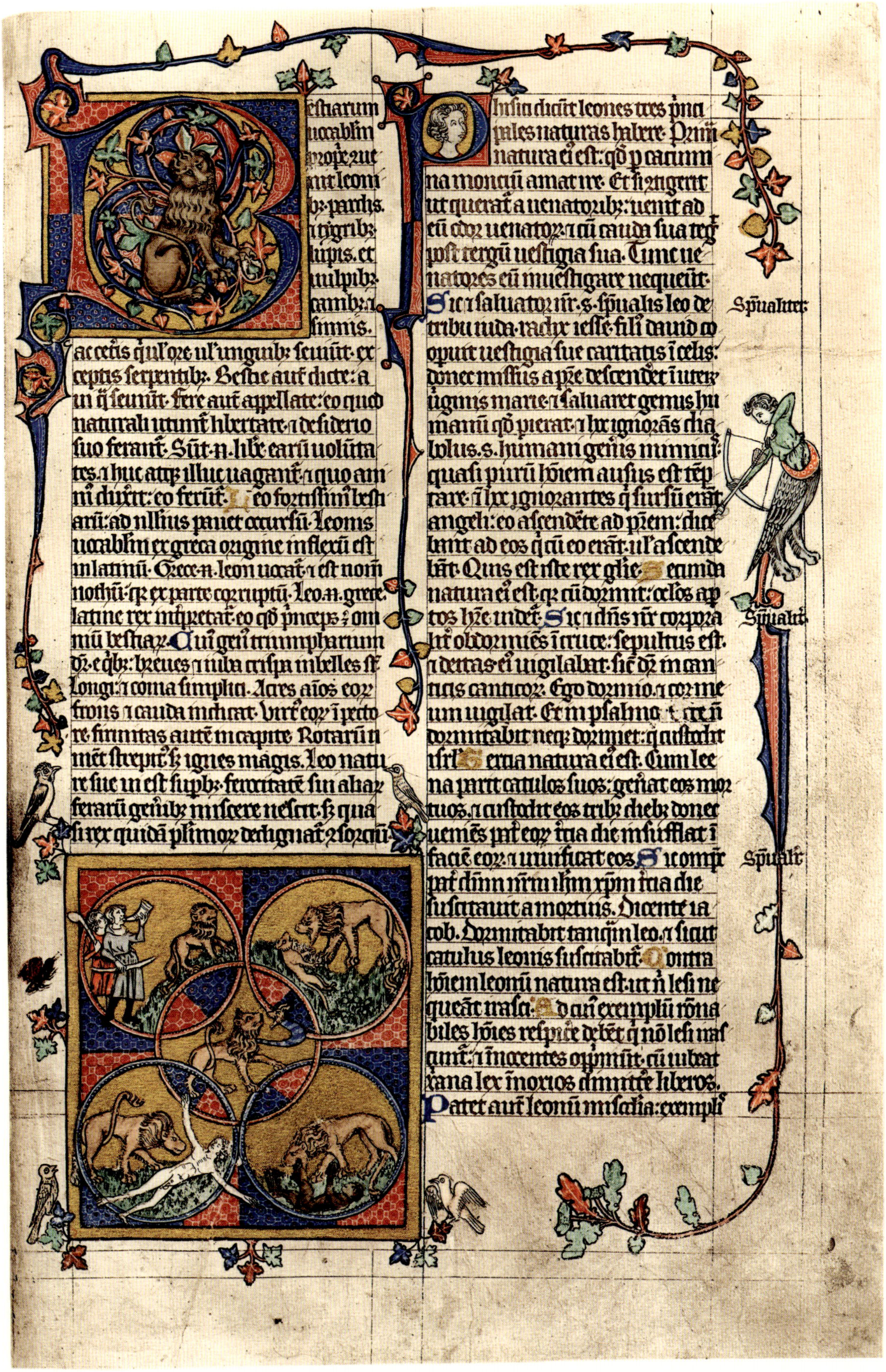

Fig. 14

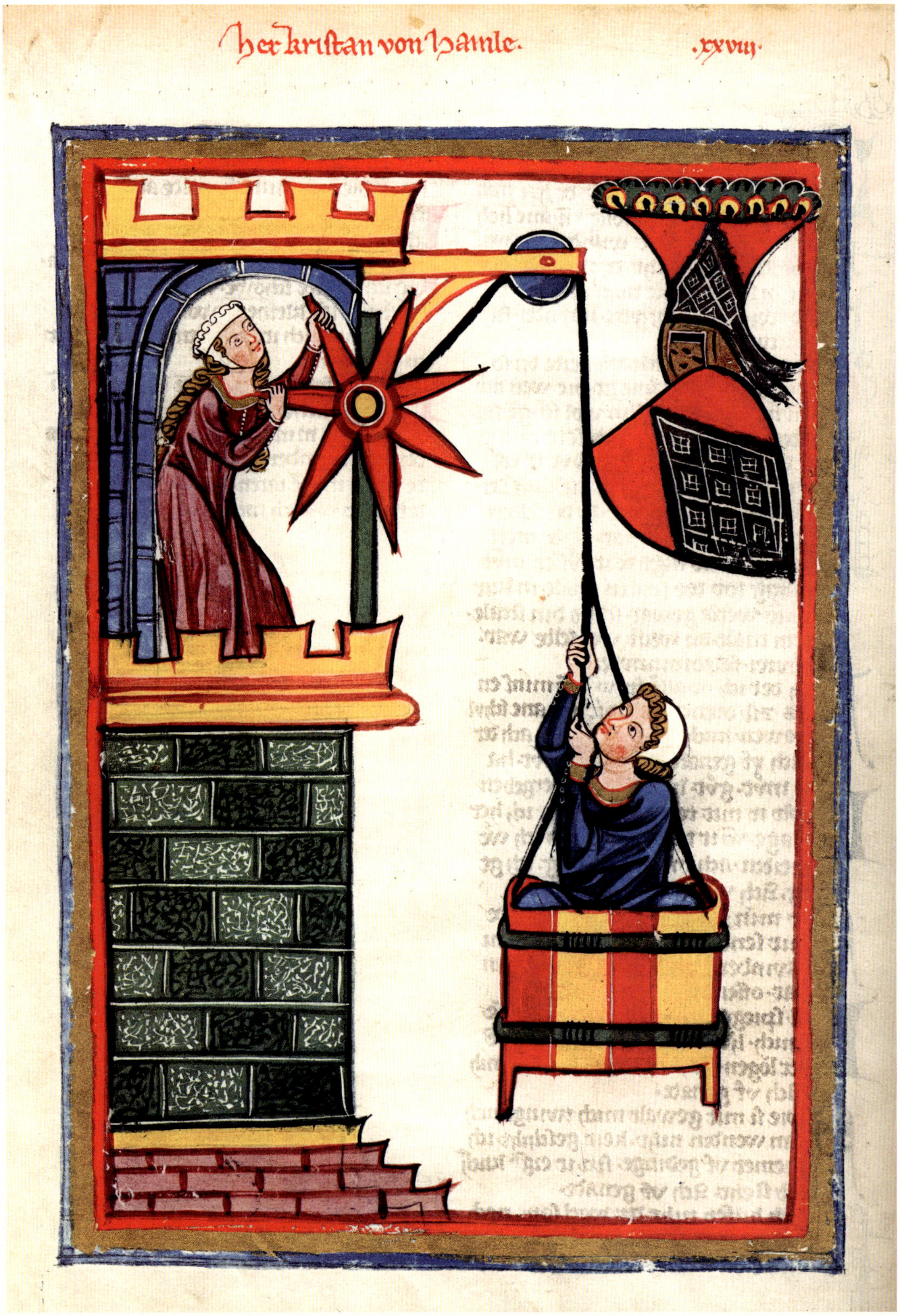

Fig. 15

26. The Codex Manesse, or the Grand Heidelberg Songbook

Manuscript: Heidelberg, Universitätsbibliothek, Cod. Pal. germ. 848.

Produced in Zurich for the Manesse family; the main portion was completed ca. 1305, and significant additions were made ca. 1340.

Parchment; 426 leaves; 35.0 x 25.0 cm.

Decorated; 137 miniatures (full-page).

Principal contents:

Some 6,000 songs by approximately 140 Minnesänger, many of them being noble or even royal personages.

Facsimiles on display:

1) *Die Manessische Lieder-Handschrift: Faksimile-Ausgabe*. Ed. Rudolf Sillib, Friedrich Panzer, and Arthur Haseloff. 2 vols. Leipzig: Insel-Verlag, 1929.

2) *Die Minnesinger in Bildern der Manessischen Handschrift*. Fwd. Hans Naumann. Leipzig: Insel-Verlag, [1933?].

THE CODEX MANESSE is a wonderful and most important collection of German troubadour songs, and the illustrations accompanying the songs provide quite a full guide to an idealized view of the conduct of the life and love affairs of a nobleman (what is often, though somewhat misleadingly, called "courtly love"). The contents of the work are ordered according to the social rank of the poets, beginning with the love songs of the Holy Roman Emperor, Henry VI, followed by a variety of kings, dukes, other noblemen, and commoners. The miniatures portray the poets whose songs are in the collection; some of the illustrations focus on the poets' heraldic devices, and others represent the poets in romantic situations similar to those in their songs.

A complete facsimile of the manuscript has also been published on DVD by the Universitätsbibliothek Heidelberg. The miniatures showing the various poets can be viewed online at <http://digi.ub.uni-heidelberg.de/cpg848>.

In one of the two images displayed, f. 71v, we see the poet-knight-lover, Herr Kristan von Hamle (fl. ca. 1210), being lifted to his lady's room in a tub by means of an elaborate pulley system. The engineering that was involved is depicted in detail and was probably intended to be humorous; certainly the idea that the lady could keep such an apparatus hidden from her husband seems absurd. Herr Kristan, though a brave warrior, here appears rather nervously clutching the rope as he hangs suspended between earth and the "heaven" of his lady's bedroom, and he seems aware that he is at her mercy should she decide to "reject" him and allow him to fall.

In the other image, f. 202v, Konrad von Suonegge (fl. ca. 1230) is seen hunting. While such a hunt is certainly part of the life of every nobleman, there may be a further significance to the choice of subject for the picture. According to one of his poems, the one who brings down the stag "will kiss whichever maiden of them all he most desires," so the stag hunt here may also be a metaphor for the "hunt" which is love (cf. the juxtaposition of bedroom and hunting scenes in *Gawain and the Green Knight*). ❋

Codex Manesse / Die grosse Heidelberger Liederhandschrift: Kommentar zum Faksimile des Codex Palatinus Germanicus 848 der Universitätsbibliothek Heidelberg. Ed. Walter Koschorreck and Wilfried Werner. Kassel: Graphische Anstalt für Kunst und Wissenschaft Ganymed, 1981.

27. Carmina Burana, or the Beuern Songbook

Manuscript: Munich, Bayerische Staatsbibliothek, Clm. 4660.

Produced in Bavaria or Austria, ca. 1320–1330.

Parchment; 112 + 7 leaves; 25.0 x 17.0 cm.

Little decoration: some rubrication and initials in red penwork; 8 miniatures (1 full-page).

Script: Protogothic book script (three scribes).

Facsimiles on display:

1) *Carmina Burana: Bayerische Staatsbibliothek, München, Clm 4660 + 4660a*. Ed. Bernhard Bischoff. 2 vols. Munich: Prestel Verlag, 1967.

2) *Carmina Burana: Facsimile Reproduction of the Manuscript Clm 4660 and Clm 4660a (Bayerische Staatsbibliothek, München)*. Ed. Bernhard Bischoff. 2 vols. Publications of Mediaeval Musical Manuscripts 9. New York: Institute of Mediaeval Music, [1967].

This is an important collection of some 1,000 songs, mostly in Latin, but with some in German, and one of the principal collections of medieval Goliardic verse. The collection was arranged thematically into sections: religious songs (now lost), moral and satirical songs (many on avarice and clerical simony), love songs (the largest section), and songs of drinking and gaming; there are also texts for several religious dramas. The songs are on such themes as the mutability of fortune, the joys and sorrows of love, and the pleasures and dangers of gambling. The fact that they are mostly in Latin and that they echo classical models suggests that they are written by people well educated, associated with the universities; further, the fact that some of the songs are rather rude and scandalous, even irreligious and blasphemous, suggests that they were "off hours" amusements of undergraduates (who were, by definition in those days, in training for careers in the Church). Given these facts, Bischoff's introduction suggests that, although the manuscript was long in the library of the Abbey of Benediktbeuern (which gives the manuscript its name), it is unlikely that it originated there; rather, the manuscript was probably compiled in the court of some prelate who was a patron of students.

Some of the lyrics are accompanied by neumes (as can be seen on the first page, on display), indicating musical settings; these are, then, "songs" and not just lyric poems. The collection will be best known to audiences of modern choral music, however, as the source of the cantata "Carmina Burana" by Carl Orff (composed 1935–1936), which presents 24 of the songs from this manuscript in modern settings.

The opening page of the manuscript (f. 1r), also on display, includes an image of Fortune's wheel, upon which can be seen four royal figures, labelled, respectively, *regnabo* ("I will reign"), *regno* ("I reign"), *regnavi* ("I reigned"), and *sum fine regno* ("I am finished reigning"). These labels illustrate the principal tenses of the Latin verb, such as a student would have had to memorize and recite repeatedly, as well as the idea of changeable Fortune.

The last six lines on this page are the words to the song "O Fortuna," which features prominently in Orff's cantata:

O Fortuna
velut luna
statu variabilis,
semper crescis
aut decrescis....

O Fortune,
like the moon
you are changeable,
ever waxing
and waning....

The second copy of the facsimile is open to some of the songs of gaming (ff. 91v–92r), and the miniatures here show two common medieval games being played, backgammon and chess. ✲

Lehtonen, Tuomas M.S. *Fortuna, Money, and the Sublunar World: Twelfth-Century Ethical Poetics and the Satirical Poetry of the "Carmina Burana."* Bibliotheca historica 9. Helsinki: Finnish Historical Society, 1995.

28. The Hours of Jeanne d'Évreux

Manuscript: New York, Metropolitan Museum of Art, Cloisters Collection.
Produced in France, 1324–1328.
Fine vellum; 209 leaves; 8.9 x 6.2 cm.
Decorated; historiated initials; numerous miniatures.
Script: Gothic bookhand ("black letter"; "littera textualis formata").
Artist: Jean Pucelle.
Facsimile on display: *The Hours of Jeanne d'Évreux, Queen of France, at the Cloisters, the Metropolitan Museum of Art*. Intro. J.J. Rorimer. New York: Metropolitan Museum of Art, 1957.

THIS PARTICULAR BOOK OF HOURS was commissioned by Charles IV (d. 1328) as a gift for his wife, Jeanne d'Évreux (d. 1371), and seems to have been completed in the mid 1320s. It is exceptionally small and delicate: the facsimile enlarges the book by one third, and even so it is quite tiny. The book was commissioned from Jean Pucelle, who is said to have used no assistants on this project, but every pen and brush stroke in this manuscript is his. Pucelle was quite a famous illuminator in his time (and since), and is said to have led some major changes in French manuscript illumination: he largely abandoned gold-leaf backdrops, and developed techniques of fine drawing, including the careful modelling of drapery and of rounded surfaces. The miniatures in this manuscript are primarily grisaille ("shades of grey," though with touches of colour), and Pucelle is credited with creating a fashion for grisaille in later French manuscripts (Avril 15).

In the next century, this manuscript was owned by Jean duc de Berry (whose name is associated with Items 38 to 40 in this exhibition), whose inventory describes it as "a small Book of Hours of Our Lady, called the Hours of Pucelle" (Rorimer 8; cf. Avril 14). In an age of anonymous artists, it is remarkable that even after a century Pucelle's name could add value for a collector of fine books. Several of the "drolleries" and "grotesques" (mostly animals or lower class people doing "lower class" activities) which appear in the margins of the Duc de Berry's "Grandes heures" appear to be modelled upon ones found in this manuscript (Avril 34).

The website of the Cloisters, the medieval department of the Metropolitan Museum of Art, includes an "explore and learn" page based on this manuscript: <http://www.metmuseum.org/explore/Jde/jdesplash.htm>.

The opening on display (ff. 102v–103r) is the beginning of the Office of St. Louis (King Louis X, canonized in 1297, and whose Psalter appears in this exhibition). The Office of St. Louis is not common in Books of Hours, but the royal family of France, as noted above (Item 23), promoted the cult of St. Louis. In the image on the left, we see Jeanne d'Évreux kneeling in a small chapel with a prayer book (perhaps this Book of Hours) open before her; the chapel in which she kneels affords her a view of the tomb of her great grandfather, St. Louis, which was in the church of the Abbey of Saint-Denis. The tomb, upon which stands a statue of St. Louis, is guarded by two soldiers (note the visible hilt of a sword, which ordinarily would be forbidden within a sacred place) to prevent the theft of the relics. Popular piety and the desire among religious houses to gain prestige led with some frequency to the theft of sacred relics, and it is known that the monks of Saint-Denis had hired soldiers to prevent the loss of the relics of St. Louis (Avril 53). Note the attempt to represent the interior space with a certain sense of visual perspective; also note below the images the "drolleries" which support them.

The image on the facing page is the first of a sequence of eight scenes from the life of St. Louis, this representing his education: the king, in saintly humility, submits to the chastisement of his confessor. ✲

Avril, François. *Manuscript Painting at the Court of France: The Fourteenth Century, 1310–1380*. Trans. Ursule Molinaro. New York: George Braziller, 1978.

29. The Luttrell Psalter

Manuscript: London, British Library, Addit. MSS 42130 and 42131.
Produced in England, ca. 1340.
Fine vellum; 309 leaves; 36.0 x 24.5 cm.
Luxuriously decorated, including miniatures in the bottom margins of most pages, and many drolleries in the side margins.
Script: Gothic bookhand ("black letter"; "littera textualis formata").
Facsimile on display: *The Luttrell Psalter: A Facsimile*. Commentary by Michelle P. Brown. London: British Library, 2006.

THIS PSALTER was done for Sir Geoffrey Luttrell (d. 1345), of Irnham, Lincolnshire, who was one of the great lords in the north, with extensive estates in Lincolnshire and Yorkshire. Sir Geoffrey himself is represented in one of the many miniatures in the manuscript. On f. 202v we see a mounted knight, bearing the arms of the Luttrells, being given a helmet by a lady wearing a gown showing the arms of Luttrell impaling Sutton (to identify Geoffrey's wife, Agnes Sutton), and being given a shield by a lady wearing a gown showing the arms of Luttrell impaling Scope of Masham (his daughter-in-law, Beatrice le Scope); above this is written "Dominus Galfridus Louterell me fieri fecit" ("The Lord Geoffrey Luttrell caused me to be made").

Some 200 of the manuscript's 309 leaves include miniatures and marginal drolleries, and the range of subjects illustrated is of considerable interest. There are scenes from the legends of saints and from the life of Christ, juxtaposed with scenes of ordinary life (from birth to death, in town and country, among rich and poor, at work and play). In one sequence, for example, an image of the lord and family at feast is accompanied by further images showing the kitchens and the feast being prepared: such a "downstairs" view of the life of the nobility is quite uncommon in medieval art. The Luttrell Psalter, then, is a valuable encyclopedia of "medieval life."

The opening displayed, ff. 172v–173r, shows two miniatures from a sequence showing peasants at the harvest. On the left we see reaping and the binding of sheaves; on the right, the stacking of the sheaves. ✲

Backhouse, Janet. *The Luttrell Psalter*. London: British Library, 1989.
Camille, Michael. *Mirror in Parchment: The Luttrell Psalter and the Making of Medieval England*. Chicago: University of Chicago Press, 1998.

30. The Gough Map

Manuscript: Oxford, Bodleian Library, MS Gough Gen. Top. 16.
Produced in England, ca. 1360.
Parchment; 115.5 x 55.8 cm.
Facsimile on display: *The Map of Great Britain circa A.D. 1360 known as The Gough Map*. Intro. E.J.S. Parsons. London: Royal Geographical Society, 1958.

UNLIKE THE HEREFORD MAP, the Gough Map might have some utility as a navigational guide, as it is the oldest surviving map of Great Britain to include roads. Routes between towns and villages are marked in red, and close inspection will show that Roman numerals have been used to record distances. Though the origin and provenance of the map are more or less a mystery, the Gough Map (which orients east to the top) represents an important step in the history of English cartography, a transition between the Matthew Paris maps of the middle of the thirteenth century, and the Sebastian Münster and George Lily maps of the sixteenth century.

The section of the map on display shows London and the region around it. ✻

Bodleian Library. "The Gough Map." <http://www.bodley.ox.ac.uk/guides/maps/goughmap.htm>.

"The Gough Map" (with zoomable viewer). <http://143.117.30.60/website/GoughMap/viewer.htm>.

Millea, Nick. *The Gough Map: The Earliest Road Map of Great Britain*. Treasures from the Bodleian Library, Oxford. Oxford: Bodleian Library Publications, 2005.

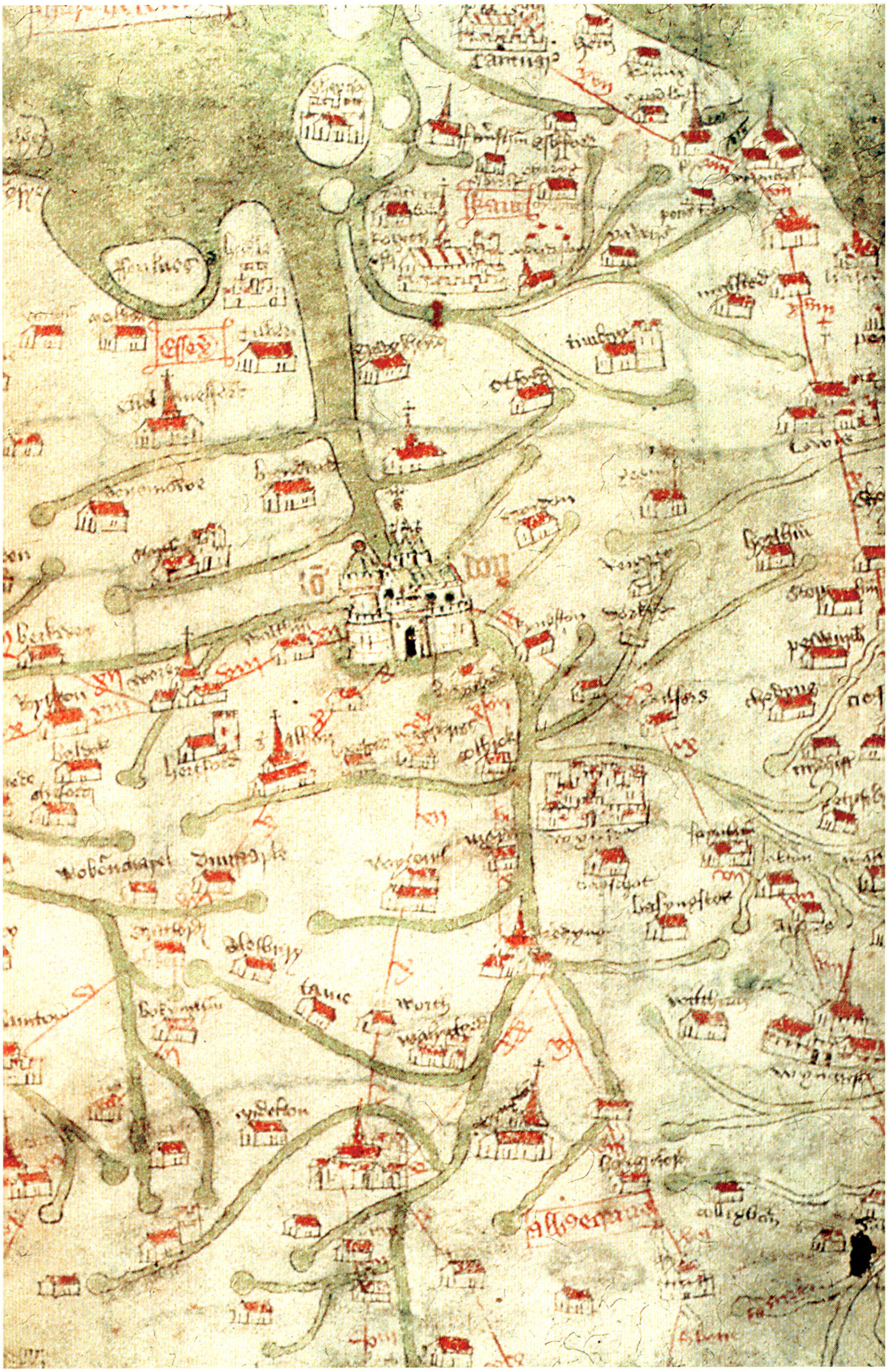

Fig. 16

31. The Visconti Psalter and Hours

Manuscripts: Florence, Biblioteca nazionale centrale di Firenze, MSS Banco Rari (BR) 397 and Landau-Finaly (LF) 22.

Produced in Italy, 1388–ca.1430.

MS BR 397 (the Psalter and a collection of hymns): Fine vellum; 151 leaves; 24.7 x 15.1 cm.

Decorated and illuminated; many ornate capitals; 26 historiated initials; 11 full-page miniatures.

Script: Gothic bookhand ("black letter"; "littera textualis formata").

Scribe: "Frater Amadeus," who signed his name on f. 108r (his name also appears in a manuscript in Glasgow).

Remained in the Visconti family until 1969, when it was acquired by the Biblioteca.

MS LF 22 (a Book of Hours): Fine vellum; 167 leaves; 25.0 x 17.9 cm.

Decorated and illuminated; many ornate capitals; 31 historiated initials; 20 full-page miniatures.

Separated from its fellow in the 18th century; given to the commune of Florence in 1945 by Baron Horace Finaly.

Facsimile on display: *The Visconti Hours, National Library, Florence*. Ed. Millard Meiss and Edith W. Kirsch. New York: George Braziller, 1972.

By the end of the fourteenth century, Psalters were no longer common as lay prayer books, so the combination here of a Book of Hours with a full Psalter makes the Visconti prayer book rather unusual. Commissioned in 1388 by Gian Galeazzo Visconti, probably to celebrate the birth of his first son and heir, the decoration of the book was begun in the workshop of the artist Giovannino dei Grassi, but the work was left incomplete at the artist's death in 1398. The decoration was completed in the 1430s by Luchino Belbello, probably commissioned by Gian Galeazzo's second son, Filippo Maria Visconti.

Though now in two volumes, the work was conceived as a unit, as is evident from the similarity of size, script, and style of decoration. There is also a pictorial life of the Virgin which begins in the one and ends in the other (Kirsch, "Psalter-Hours," 41). The separation of the book into two parts probably reflects the periods of work upon it in two workshops. The BR manuscript shows no traces of the Belbello artists, so BR was essentially complete when Giovannini died; it is LF that was sent to Belbello for further work, and BR may have been bound while LF was still awaiting completion (Kirsch, "Psalter-Hours," 42).

On display is the opening of ff. 10v–11r in the LF manuscript, at the beginning of the hour of Lauds in the Office of the Virgin; it was common in Books of Hours that this position was illustrated with a miniature of the visitation of the Virgin Mary to her cousin Elizabeth, to share with her the news of the coming Incarnation, and such an image is seen here on the left. When Elizabeth greets Mary she feels her own baby (John the Baptist) leap in her womb, and thereby she recognizes that Mary is, indeed, the Mother of God. We have chosen to include a number of "Visitation" scenes in this exhibition (cf. Items 32, 47, 48, 53, 54, and 60) since it is particularly interesting to compare the backgrounds in these pictures, partly to see the gradual development of landscape painting in the later Middle Ages, but also because they offer idealized views of the medieval world: free of labour and strife, free of visible signs of lordship or competition, such landscapes presumably represent the earth returned to a paradisiacal state.

On the right, within the gold border, is the scene of the Nativity, with the familiar elements of the stall, the ox, and the ass. Mother Mary holds out the baby Jesus to one of two midwives (a second is seen below, pouring water into a bowl). Joseph makes himself useful by warming at a fire some cloths with which to swaddle the baby. Outside of the frame we see, at the top, God and angels in heaven, while, below, we see shepherds in a forest, with an angel in each side margin announcing to the shepherds the good news of Jesus' birth. ❋

Kirsch, Edith W. "The Psalter-Hours in Florence." In her *Five Illuminated Manuscripts of Giangaleazzo Visconti*. Monographs on the Fine Arts 46. University Park: Pennsylvania State University Press, for the College Art Association of America, 1991. 39–67 and 87–92.

32. The Vernon Manuscript

Manuscript: Oxford, Bodleian Library, MS Eng. poet. a.1.

Produced in England, probably in Warwickshire or N. Worcestershire (perhaps from Bordesley Abbey), ca. 1390.

Parchment; 412 leaves; 57.0 x 39.5 cm.

Decorated and illuminated; many ornate capitals; 15 miniatures.

Script: Anglicana formata, in a careful and lovely hand.

Facsimile on display: *The Vernon Manuscript: A Facsimile of Bodleian Library, Oxford, MS. Eng. poet. a.1.* Intro. A.I. Doyle. Cambridge, and Wolfeboro, NH: D.S. Brewer, 1987.

THIS IS A HUGE VOLUME, preserving a library of some 130 texts in Middle English, with a few in Latin and Anglo-French; it is much too large and too heavy (weighing ca. 20 kg.) for ordinary reading without a supporting table or bookstand, so may have been intended as something of a "repository" of texts, from which reading copies could be made. The Simeon Manuscript (London, British Library, Addit. MS 22283) is a "sister" to the Vernon Manuscript: it is of similar size (slightly taller), but with fewer texts; the texts that are there, however, seem for the most part to have been copied from the Vernon Manuscript, and many of them copied by the same scribe, so the two manuscripts are closely related and often discussed together. They are, by any standard, impressive books, and, as A.I. Doyle notes in the Introduction to the Vernon Manuscript facsimile, this pair of manuscripts "represent an exceptional enterprise of book-production for any era, by reason both of the cost of material resources devoted to them and of the time and trouble which must have been involved in assembling the contents" (Doyle 1).

The contents are primarily of a religious and devotional nature: collections of saints' lives, devotional poems, mystical treatises, and moral and didactic stories. Among the more significant works are a version of *Piers Plowman* by William Langland (a contemporary of Geoffrey Chaucer of the late fourteenth century); the *South English Legendary* (a collection of saints' lives in English verse); a series of hymns to the Virgin; *La estoire del Evangelie* (a harmonized version of the gospel story, in English verse despite its French title; this portion of the manuscript includes miniatures illustrating the gospel stories); *The Prick of Conscience*; an English version of *The Castle of Love* by Robert Grosseteste; several works by the mystic Richard Rolle and his followers; and the *Ancrene Riwle* (the Rule for Anceresses), among many other texts.

A project to produce a facsimile edition on DVD, with photographs of each page of the manuscript linked to transcriptions and commentary, is on-going. The proposed edition is described at the project website: <http://www.english.bham.ac.uk/medievalstudies/vernon/>.

The opening on display shows ff. 104v–105r, being, on the left, the end of the "Smaller Vernon Collection" of saints' lives, and, on the right, the opening of *La estoire del Evangelie*. The *Estoire* is illustrated, and there are three miniatures here: the Visitation of Mary to Elizabeth, the Annunciation (Gabriel announces the coming Incarnation to the Virgin Mary), and Zacharias (priest, and husband of Elizabeth, cousin to Mary) meeting the angel. (Zacharias, who doubted the angel's message that his aging wife would bear a child, who would be John the Baptist, was, for his scepticism, struck dumb until the birth.) ✲

The Minor Poems of the Vernon MS. Ed. C. Horstmann and F.J. Furnivall. 2 vols. Early English Text Society OS 98 and 117. London: Kegan Paul, Trench, Trübner and Co., for the Early English Text Society, 1892–1901.

Scott, Kathleen L. *Later Gothic Manuscripts, 1390–1490*. 2 vols. A Survey of Manuscripts Illuminated in the British Isles 6. London: Harvey Miller Publishers, 1996. 1: 19–24 (Item 1), and Ills. 2–5 and Pl. 3.

Studies in the Vernon Manuscript. Ed. Derek Pearsall. Cambridge: D.S. Brewer, 1990.

33. The Pearl Manuscript

Manuscript: London, British Library, MS Cotton Nero A.x, art. 3.

Produced in East Cheshire; late fourteenth century (the miniatures are perhaps fifty years later).

Parchment; 90 leaves; 17.1 x 12.1 cm.

Decoration: some penwork elaboration of initial letters; 12 full-page miniatures.

Script: A rounded Gothic hand with Anglicana features.

Facsimile on display: *Pearl, Cleanness, Patience and Sir Gawain, Reproduced in Facsimile from the Unique MS. Cotton Nero A.x in the British Museum*. Intro. I. Gollancz. Early English Text Society OS 162. London: Oxford University Press, for the Early English Text Society, 1923.

THE SMALL SIZE and unprepossessing appearance of this manuscript belies its importance to literary history, for it is the unique manuscript copy of two of the greatest Middle English poems, "Pearl" and "Gawain and the Green Knight." Because of the manuscript's small size, and the scribe's desire to make full use of the space available to him (there are approximately 36 lines of verse on each small page), the writing is rather cramped and difficult to read, which is made worse by serious fading and signs of wear. The four poems of the manuscript are commonly (though not without dispute) thought to be works of a single author who, for lack of a name, is usually designated as the "Pearl-poet" or "Gawain-poet." "Pearl" and "Gawain and the Green Knight" are each accompanied by four full-page miniatures, "Patience" and "Cleanness" by two each, the miniatures having been added to the manuscript at a later date. Nothing else is known of the early history of the manuscript before it first came to notice in the seventeenth-century catalogue of the collections of Henry Saville of Banke, from whom it passed to Sir Robert Cotton by 1621, and Cotton's books became one of the founding collections of the library of the British Museum (now British Library).

Murray McGillivray at the University of Calgary is producing a hypertext edition of the four poems of the manuscript, producing a new facsimile with digital colour photographs, each of which will be linked to transcriptions and commentary. A full description of the project can be found on the project website: <http://www.ucalgary.ca/~scriptor/cotton/>.

On display is a monochrome facsimile from the early twentieth century (the images reproduce the pages of the manuscript at their original size). The opening displayed is ff. 90v–91r, showing the opening lines of "Gawain and the Green Knight." Facing the text is a miniature illustrating one of the early scenes of the story, showing the Green Knight being beheaded by Sir Gawain at King Arthur's New Year's feast. The Green Knight then, rather monstrously, picks up his head and reminds Sir Gawain that they are to meet again in a year's time. Also on display is a colour version of this "beheading of the Green Knight" miniature, as well as a second illustration to the story, in which Lady Bertilak comes to Gawain's bedroom with designs on his virtue. ✻

Edwards, A.S.G. "The Manuscript: British Library MS Cotton Nero A.x." In *A Companion to the "Gawain"-Poet*. Ed. Derek Brewer and Jonathan Gibson. Arthurian Studies 38. Cambridge: D.S. Brewer, 1997. 197–219.

Scott, Kathleen L. *Later Gothic Manuscripts, 1390–1490*. 2 vols. A Survey of Manuscripts Illuminated in the British Isles 6. London: Harvey Miller Publishers, 1996. 1: 66–68 (Item 12), and Ills. 32–35.

34. The Travels of Sir John Mandeville

Manuscript: London, British Library, Addit. MS 24189.
Produced in Bohemia (at the court of Prague), ca. 1400.
Parchment (tinted green); 16 leaves; 22.5 x 18.0 cm.
Decoration: The entire manuscript is a sequence of 28 miniatures with no accompanying text.
Facsimile on display: *The Travels of Sir John Mandeville: A Manuscript in the British Library*. Ed. Josef Krása. Trans. Peter Kussi. New York: George Braziller, 1983.

THOUGH *Mandeville's Travels* is now considered a fiction, based upon books about the wonders of the Orient from some well-stocked medieval library, it was for many centuries considered to be a true account of a real journey, and as such was one of the "best-sellers" of the later Middle Ages. The *Travels* first appeared in Latin ca. 1350, and subsequently appeared in translation in most European vernaculars. While there probably never was a Sir John Mandeville, other people in this period were in fact making trips like his: Christian pilgrims took the arduous journey to the Holy Land with some frequency; merchants in Venice and Genoa had established trade routes beyond the Holy Land into Arabia and China; and in the 1330s there were at least two groups of Franciscan friars who followed those trade routes to take Christianity to China.

This manuscript is a series of 28 miniatures with no text, so some scholarly "detective" work was necessary to identify these as illustrations to the early chapters of Mandeville's story. The artist used an unusual technique of semi-grisaille painting on green-tinted vellum, which produces quite a dramatic visual effect. The illustrations are also notable for the detail with which fashions in clothing of the time are represented.

Reproduced on the slipcase is Pl. 4 of the facsimile, showing Sir John Mandeville and his companions coming to Constantinople. The first part of Mandeville's journey took him from northern Europe through the Balkans to Constantinople; from there he took ship to Cyprus and then to the

Middle East, and then through Persia and India to China. Here we see the travellers in animated conversation (as is indicated by their gestures), presumably discussing the sites that they have visited along the way. A sense of depth and distance is suggested by the composition of the scene on an upward sweeping diagonal. Still, realism and "perspective" are not being sought to any great extent: the sky is blue, but decorated with floral motifs; the water is filled with massive and strange aquatic insects; and Mandeville's personal significance is indicated not only by his elegant dress and the touches of gold in its decoration, but also by the fact that he is represented at a slightly larger size than his companions.

The book is open at Pl. 25 (f. 8r), showing the travellers as they enter Syria. Mandeville's journey takes him from the Isle of Cyprus through Tyre and Jaffa on his way to Jerusalem and beyond. In this section of the book, references to Old and New Testament stories abound. This image shows two scenes: in the lower portion, Mandeville and his companions approach the city of Tyre, now in Saracen hands, and must pay a toll before entering. Later, in the upper portion, the travellers come to Jaffa, said to be named for Noah's son Japhet. Mandeville states that the city wall is decorated with a forty-foot-long rib of a giant (a corruption of a classical story of Andromeda being threatened here by a sea monster); the rib can be seen hanging from the wall. ✻

35. The Hengwrt Manuscript of the *Canterbury Tales*

Manuscript: Aberystwyth, National Library of Wales, MS Peniarth 392D (formerly Hengwrt 154).

Produced in London, ca. 1410.

Parchment; 249 leaves; ca 29.2 x 21.0 cm.

Opening page decorated; some minor decoration and flourishing elsewhere; no miniatures.

Script: Anglicana formata (Adam Pinkhurst the main scribe).

Facsimile on display: Chaucer, Geoffrey. *The Canterbury Tales: A Facsimile and Transcription of the Hengwrt Manuscript with Variants from the Ellesmere Manuscript*. Ed. Paul G. Ruggiers. Intro. Donald C. Baker, A.I. Doyle, and M.B. Parkes. A Variorum Edition of the Works of Geoffrey Chaucer I. Norman, OK: University of Oklahoma Press, 1979.

THE *Canterbury Tales* is another tale of travelling and pilgrimage, and offers an encyclopedic view of life among the inhabitants of late medieval England. The "General Prologue" tells of how "nine and twenty in a company of sundry folk" stayed one night in the Tabard Inn in Southwark, on the south side of London Bridge, intending to leave early the next morning on a pilgrimage to Canterbury, the site of the shrine of St. Thomas Becket (the twelfth-century Archbishop of Canterbury, murdered in his cathedral by knights of King Henry II). "Geoffrey" decides to join the company, and the Host of the Inn, Harry Bailey, encourages them to pass the time on the road in a tale-telling competition. The tales that the pilgrims tell are, then, the *Canterbury Tales*, and each story reveals the pilgrim-teller's views on life, love, and the world.

The Hengwrt manuscript and the Ellesmere manuscript are the two earliest copies extant of the *Canterbury Tales*, both produced by the same scribe in quick succession. The Ellesmere manuscript is a very fine, deluxe manuscript of the highest quality; the Hengwrt manuscript, by contrast, is inferior to the Ellesmere in size and quality: it is made up of smaller leaves, of lower quality parchment, with less decoration, and without miniatures. The text of the *Tales*, too, seems poorer, though this is also possibly evidence that it more closely resembles the state of Chaucer's papers at his death: thus, paradoxically, the "inferior" quality of the text may, in fact, be evidence that it is the "better" text, in the sense of being a more accurate representation of what Chaucer wrote rather than how an editor-scribe "improved" upon what Chaucer wrote.

The opening on display is the opening page of the "General Prologue" to the *Canterbury Tales* (f. 2r), showing the most elaborately decorated page of the manuscript, but one which also has suffered very considerable wear over time. ❊

Seymour, M.C. *A Catalogue of Chaucer Manuscripts*. 2 vols. Aldershot, Hants.: Scolar Press / Ashgate Publishing, 1995–1997. 2: 31–34.

Facsimile on display: Chaucer, Geoffrey. *The Hengwrt Chaucer Digital Facsimile*. (CD-ROM.) Ed. Estelle Stubbs. The Canterbury Tales Project. Leicester: Scholarly Digital Editions, 2000.

The CD-ROM facsimile of the Hengwrt Manuscript reproduces the pages of the manuscript in digital colour photographs (at 225 dpi), each image linked to a full transcription (text and glosses) and to a database of collations with the Ellesmere Manuscript's text. The manuscript pages can be viewed as individual pages, as openings, or as conjugate leaves. Stubbs argues in her introduction that parts of the Hengwrt manuscript were done before Chaucer's death, possibly overseen by Chaucer himself, which would give the Hengwrt Manuscript an even greater authority than that more commonly attributed to it.

36. The Ellesmere Manuscript of the *Canterbury Tales*

Manuscript: San Marino, CA, Huntington Library, MS EL 26.C.9.

Produced in London, ca. 1410.

Fine vellum; 232 leaves; ca. 39.5 x 28.0 cm.

Decorated and illuminated; over 70 leaves have border decoration; 23 miniatures.

Script: Anglicana formata (Adam Pinkhurst the main scribe).

Facsimile on display: Chaucer, Geoffrey. *The "Canterbury Tales": The New Ellesmere Chaucer Facsimile (of Huntington Library MS EL 26 C 9)*. Ed. Daniel Woodward and Martin Stevens. San Marino: Huntington Library; Tokyo: Yushodo, 1995.

THE ELLESMERE MANUSCRIPT is a beautiful example of late medieval book production; it is, as noted in the previous entry, roughly contemporary with, and from the same workshop as, the Hengwrt Manuscript. The Ellesmere Manuscript's text of the *Canterbury Tales* is the one that is usually used as the base text for modern editions of the work, though there are a number of Chaucer editors who argue that the Hengwrt Manuscript better represents the somewhat chaotic state of Chaucer's working papers at the time of his death, and that the "superiority" of the Ellesmere Manuscript's text is the product of posthumous editing (thus not "authorial" but "scribal").

The manuscript is beautifully decorated, with many coloured capital letters, and many pages decorated with floral borders in colours and gold-leaf. There are also 23 miniatures, being equestrian portraits of those pilgrims who tell tales, each teller depicted alongside the opening lines of the tale told. The horses upon which they sit reflect the social status and condition of the riders: the poor scholar, for instance, rides a horse that is so poorly fed that its ribs are showing. The opening displayed (ff. 153v–154r) includes the end of "Geoffrey's" failed tale of Sir Thopas (cut off by the Host as "drasty rhyming") and the beginning of his second attempt, a prose tale, concerning Melibee and his wife, Dame Prudence. The portrait here is not unlike other extant representations of Geoffrey Chaucer, such as the painting that hangs in the National Portrait

Gallery. Chaucer wears a belted gown, a "liripipe" hat (distinguishable by its long tail), and has the casing for his pencil or stylus on his breast (like an iconographic symbol identifying the person or the office: he is "writer"). The perspective is somewhat problematic, for there seems to have been insufficient room to provide him with an adequate horse. ✻

Dutschke, C.W., with the assistance of R.H. Rouse, et al. *Guide to Medieval and Renaissance Manuscripts in the Huntington Library*. 2 vols. San Marino, CA: Huntington Library, 1989. 1: 41–50.

The Ellesmere Chaucer: Essays in Interpretation. Ed. Martin Stevens and Daniel Woodward. San Marino, CA: Huntington Library; Tokyo: Yushodo, 1995.

Scott, Kathleen L. *Later Gothic Manuscripts, 1390–1490*. 2 vols. A Survey of Manuscripts Illuminated in the British Isles 6. London: Harvey Miller Publishers, 1996. 1: 140–43 (Item 42), and Ills. 176–80.

Seymour, M.C. *A Catalogue of Chaucer Manuscripts*. 2 vols. Aldershot, Hants.: Scolar Press / Ashgate Publishing, 1995–1997. 2: 230–35.

Stevens, Martin. "The Ellesmere Miniatures as Illustrations of Chaucer's *Canterbury Tales*." *Studies in Iconography* 7–8 (1981–1982): 113–34.

Thorpe, James. *Chaucer's "Canterbury Tales": The Ellesmere Manuscript*. 2nd ed. San Marino, CA: Huntington Library, 1978.

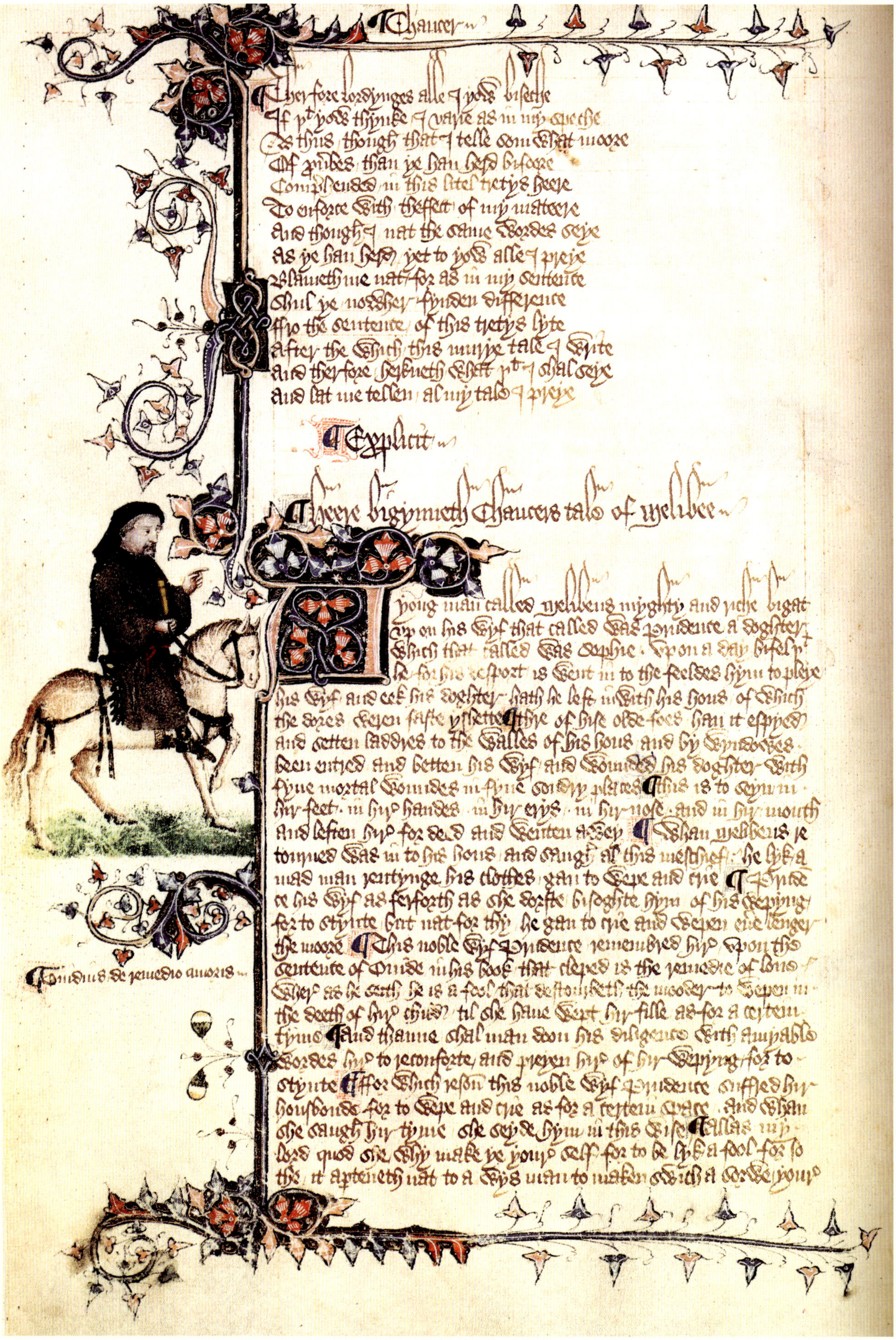

Fig. 17

doghter with the grace of god shal warisshe and escape and al were it
so that she right now were deed ye ne oughte nat as for hir deeth
youre self to destroye ¶ Senek seith the wise man shal nat take to ¶ Seneca
greet disconfort for the deeth of his children but certes he sholde suf
fren it in pacience as wel as he abideth the deeth of his owene
propre persone ¶ This Melibeus answerde anon and seyde ¶ What man ¶ Melibeus
quod he sholde of his wepyng stente that hath so greet a cause for to
wepe Jhesu crist oure lord hym self wepte for the deeth of Lazarus hys ¶ Qualiter Jhesus xpc flevit pro morte Lazari
freend ¶ Prudence answerde certes wel I woot attempree we ¶ Prudence
pyng is no thyng deffended to hym þt sorweful is amonges folk in
sorwe but it is rather graunted hym to wepe ¶ The apostle paul ¶ Apostolus paulus ad Romanos
un to the Romayns writeth man shal rejoyse with hem that make
joye and wepen with swich folk as wepen ¶ But though attempree
wepyng be ygraunted outrageous wepyng certes is deffended mesure
of wepyng sholde be considered after the lore þt techeth us Senek
¶ Whan that thy freend is deed quod he lat nat thyne eyen to moyste been ¶ Seneca
of teeris ne to muche drye Al though the teeris come to thyne eyen lat
hem nat falle and whan thou hast for goon thy freend do diligence
to gete another freend and this is moore wysdom than for to wepe
for thy freend which that thou hast lorn for ther inne is no boote
And therfore if ye governe yow by sapience put awey sorwe out of
youre herte ¶ Remembre yow þt Jhesus Syrak seith ¶ A man that is ¶ Jhesus Syrak
joyous and glad in herte it hym conserveth florisshynge in his age
But soothly sorweful herte maketh hise bones drye ¶ He seith eek
thus that sorwe in herte sleeth ful many a man ¶ Salomon seith
that right as motthes in the shepes flees anoyeth to the clothes & ¶ Salomon
the smale wormes to the tree right so anoyeth sorwe to the herte wher
fore us oghte as wel in the deeth of oure children as in the losse of oure
goodes temporels have pacience ¶ Remembre yow upon the pacient ¶ Vide Job
Job whan he hadde lost his children and his temporel substance and
in his body endured and receyved ful many a grevous tribulacion yet
seyde he thus ¶ Oure lord hath yeve it me right as oure lord hath wold
right so it is doon blessed be the name of oure lord ¶ To thise forseide
thynges answerde Melibeus un to his wyf Prudence ¶ Alle thy wor ¶ Melibeus
des quod he been sothe and ther with profitable but trewely myn herte
is troubled with this sorwe so grevously that I noot what to doone
¶ Lat calle quod Prudence thy trewe freendes alle and thy lynage whi ¶ Prudence
che that been wise telleth youre cas and herkneth what they seye in
conseillyng and yow governe after hir sentence ¶ Salomon seith werk ¶ Salomon
alle thy thynges by conseil and thou shalt never repente ¶ Thanne by
the conseil of his wyf Prudence this Melibeus leet callen a greet con
gregacion of folk as surgiens phisiciens olde folk and yonge and so
me of hise olde enemys reconsiled as by hir semblaunt to his love and
in to his grace and ther with al ther coomen somme of hise neighebores
that diden hym reverence moore for drede than for love as it happeth ofte
¶ Ther coomen also ful many subtille flatereres and wise advocatz ler
ned in the lawe And whan this folk togidre assembled weren this Me
libeus in sorweful wise shewed hem his cas and by the manere of his

37. The Paris *Livre de la chasse*

Manuscript: Paris, Bibliothèque nationale de France, Ms. français 616.
Produced in Paris, ca. 1410.
Fine vellum; 214 leaves (the first ten are modern); 35.7 x 25.0 cm.
Decorated and illuminated; ornate initials; 87 miniatures.
Script: Gothic bookhand ("black letter"; "littera textualis formata").
Artist: possibly an associate of the "Master of the Duke of Bedford."
Principal contents:

1) Livre de la chasse (ff. 11r–121v) [ff. 1r–10v are modern paper leaves, with items related to later owners, and information about the manuscript].
2) Prayers in Latin and French (ff. 122r–138r).
3) Les Déduits de la chasse par Gace de la Buigne (ff. 139r–214r; added at a later date; not included in the facsimile).

Facsimile on display: Gaston III Phœbus, Count of Foix. *Le livre de la chasse / Das Buch von der Jagd: vollständige Faksimile-Ausgabe im Originalformat des Manuscrit français 616 der Bibliothèque nationale, Paris*. Commentary Marcel Thomas, François Avril, and Pierre Herzog von Brissac. Trans. (of the text of the manuscript into Modern French) Robert Bossuat and André Bossuat. 2 vols. Codices selecti phototypice impressi 53. Graz: Akademische Druck- u. Verlagsanstalt, 1976.

GASTON PHÉBUS (1331–1391), count of Foix and viscount of Béarn, completed in 1389 his *Livre de la chasse*, a guide to the aristocratic art of hunting or of "venery." The book describes the various types of prey and their typical behaviours, from the noblest stag to the meanest fox and wildcat; it outlines the breeds of dogs and their peculiar talents, and explains the training and care of dogs; and it describes the various types of the hunt and the special techniques involved in each. It seems to have been a very popular work, since it is found in some forty-four extant medieval manuscripts, and was translated into a number of other languages. This particular copy, one of the earliest and most beautiful, appears to have been commissioned by Philip the Bold, Duke of Burgundy, and brother of the bibliophile Duc de Berry.

It was produced in a Parisian atelier, possibly by artisans associated with the "Master of the Duke of Bedford" (the miniatures here have many stylistic similarities with those of the Bedford Master, to be seen, for instance, in the Bedford Hours — now London, British Library, Addit. MS 18850 — and others).

The opening on display (ff. 115v–116r) includes two miniatures: on the left is an example of the use of a decoy (*la toile*) in the hunting of a stag; on the right, the dogs have cornered a boar, and the huntsmen prepare their crossbows to shoot it. ✼

38. The Grandes Heures of Jean Duc de Berry

Manuscript: Paris, Bibliothèque nationale de France, Ms. latin 919.

Produced in Paris, 1407–1409.

Fine vellum; 126 leaves; 40.0 x 30.0 cm.

Decorated and illuminated; historiated initials; 52 miniatures (including 5 portraits of the Duke).

Script: Gothic bookhand ("black letter"; "littera textualis formata").

Facsimile on display: *The Grandes heures of Jean, Duke of Berry, Bibliothèque nationale, Paris*. Ed. Marcel Thomas. Trans. Victoria Benedict and Benita Eisler. New York: George Braziller, 1971.

JEAN DUC DE BERRY (1340–1416) was the third son of King Jean II ("John the Good"), and so brother to King Jean's successor, Charles V, and to Louis duc d'Anjou and Philippe duc de Bourgogne ("Philip the Bold"). The Duc de Berry was one of the most wealthy men in Europe and a lover of fine things: he owned some seventeen palatial chateaus, and filled them with beautiful jewels and works of art. He was also a great collector of books and a patron of book-producing artisans, and owned at least 15 Books of Hours, 14 illuminated Bibles, 16 Psalters, 18 breviaries, and 6 missals, not to mention other books that he commissioned as gifts for others. He kept in his personal employ some of the greatest artists and craftsmen of Europe.

This exhibition includes a number of books from the Duc de Berry's collection, including the Book of Hours of Jeanne d'Évereux (Item 28). Among the books that the Duke commissioned for himself, the first included here is the "Grandes heures," so called because of its size, which approaches the upper limit for the size of leaves of parchment. It was clearly impractical for daily use but intended for display, and it makes an impressive artistic showpiece. Several artists and illuminators famous from their work on other books contributed to the creation of this one, such as the "Pseudo-Jacquemart de Hesdin" and the "Bedford Master," and the book is said to have taken several years of continuous labour to complete.

Some 438 images related to this Book of Hours are reproduced in the Bibliothèque nationale's "Mandragore" image database, <http://mandragore.bnf.fr/>.

The facsimile is open to Pls. 95–96, showing the richly decorated text. On Pl. 95, the floral border, in the upper right corner, gradually turns into a dragon. On Pl. 96, the miniature shows St. Peter with the elements of the mass on an altar; he appears to be speaking to the congregants, perhaps explaining this new ritual to early Christian converts. Descending upon them is the Holy Ghost in the form of a dove. Below this is a historiated initial with an image of Jean duc de Berry at prayer, upon whom God looks down from on high (presumably with favour). The other decorations include the Duke's coat of arms, his initials in a monogram, and his heraldic animals (bears and swans); in the lower margin are a bird in flight and a butterfly. ✲

39. The Belles Heures of Jean duc de Berry

(ALSO KNOWN AS THE HEURES D'AILLY)

Manuscript: New York, Metropolitan Museum of Art, Cloisters Collection.
Produced in Paris by Flemish artists (the Limbourg brothers), ca. 1409.
Fine vellum; 224 leaves; 23.8 x 16.8 cm.
Decorated and illuminated; 172 miniatures (94 full-page).
Script: Gothic bookhand ("black letter"; "littera textualis formata").
Facsimiles on display:

1) *The Belles heures of Jean, Duke of Berry; The Cloisters, the Metropolitan Museum of Art*. Ed. Millard Meiss and Elizabeth H. Beatson. New York: George Braziller, 1974.
2) *The Belles heures of Jean, Duke of Berry, Prince of France*. Intro. James J. Rorimer. New York: Metropolitan Museum of Art, 1958.

AMONG THE ARTISANS who were under the patronage of the Duc de Berry were the Limbourg brothers of Guelders (Pol, Herman, and Jean). They made several Books of Hours for the Duke, including this one, known as the "Belles heures" for the beauty of its decoration.

While it is common in Books of Hours for there to be pictures of saints, they usually are single icons; one interesting feature of this book is that there are several pictorial sequences of scenes from the legends of certain saints, including, for instance, a legend of St. Catherine in eleven miniatures. The first of the two facsimiles of this manuscript that we have included, then, is open to an image of St. Catherine, here seen at study. She sits at an elaborate writing desk, and nearby is a multi-layered book table, topped with a statue of Moses (recipient of the ten commandments and therefore representing the written word); he appears a second time on an altar in a chapel in the background.

The other facsimile is open to a pair of miniatures from the lives of St. Anthony and St. Paul the Hermit. On the left (Pl. 22), Anthony, in response to a vision informing him that Paul is soon to die, travels through the wilderness in search of Paul's hermitage. We see here the wild land and its wild beasts, including dragons. We are near the Red Sea (represented as being literally red in colour), upon which we see a many-oared galley. In the distance, Paul is seen at his hermitage, reading. On the right (Pl. 23), Anthony, still searching, encounters a centaur (depicted as half goat rather than half horse), from whom he asks directions. Again, other wild beasts appear, including lions and antelopes. Paul again appears, still reading outside his hermitage, but now beside an open tomb, having prepared it against his own imminent death.

The Metropolitan Museum has a webpage devoted to this manuscript: <http://www.metmuseum.org/toah/hd/manu/hod_54.1.1.htm>. ✻

Dückers, Rob, and Pieter Roelofs. *The Limbourg Brothers: Nijmegen Masters at the French Court, 1400–1416*. Nijmegen, Holland: Ludion, 2005.

40. The Très Riches Heures of Jean duc de Berry

Manuscript: Chantilly, Musée Condé, MS 65.

Produced in France by Flemish artists (the Limbourg brothers), ca. 1412–1416; completed in the 1480s (by Jean Columbe).

Fine vellum; 206 leaves; 29.0 x 21.0 cm.

Decorated and illuminated; many historiated initials; 131 miniatures (48 full-page).

Script: Gothic bookhand ("black letter"; "littera textualis formata").

Facsimile on display: *The Très riches heures of Jean, Duke of Berry, Musée Condé, Chantilly*. Intro. Jean Longnon and Raymond Cazelles. Pref. by Millard Meiss. Trans. Victoria Benedict. New York: George Braziller, 1969.

THE TRÈS RICHES HEURES is the most famous of the Duc de Berry's books. Like the Belles heures, it was done by the Limbourg brothers, and their work on this manuscript seems to have begun as soon as the Belles heures was completed. The Très riches heures, however, was left incomplete when all three of the brothers died suddenly, at less than the age of 30, more or less at the same time, in February of 1416, presumably of some contagion. There is a legend that they caught the Plague while painting a scene of Pestilence depicted as one of the Four Horsemen of the Apocalypse. The Duke himself was dead not long after (15 June), said to have died of a broken heart caused by the defeat of France (and of his royal brother) at the Battle of Agincourt the previous year. About seventy years later, the then owner of the manuscript, Charles duc de Savoie, commissioned Jean Columbe to finish the manuscript (1485–1489).

Among its most frequently reproduced images are the representations of the "labours of the months" from the Calendar. It was common in Books of Hours to illustrate the listing of saints' days and festivals for each month with images of "peasant labour" appropriate to the season, but the illustrations in the Très riches heures are so detailed and elaborate that they are remarkable paintings in and of themselves. Each has a zodiacal sky chart at the top representing the month, with a scene (most of which include one or other of the Duc de Berry's many chateaus in the background) either of peasants working at seasonal labour or of noble people occupied in some seasonal activity, such as a New Year's Feast for the month of January. These paintings were quite famous even in their own time, and were much imitated; the Calendar images in the Grimani Breviary (Item 55), for instance, are variations on these.

One curious feature of the manuscript is that four of the Limbourg's full-page miniatures are "tipped in," and thus clearly extra to the original plan for the work. Each of the four represents a subject unusual in a Book of Hours: a diagram of human anatomy ("Anatomical Man"); an image of the Garden of Eden, showing the four stages in the Fall of Man; a plan of the City of Rome; and the scene of the Fall from Heaven of the Rebel Angels. Why the artists or the Duke decided to include paintings of these particular subjects, and to add them to the book at a late stage, has caused much scholarly debate.

The Institut de France, which owns the Chateau de Chantilly of which the Musée Condé is a part, has an online exhibition of the Très riches heures: <http://www.institut-de-france.fr/animations/berry/berry.html>. They also have produced a digital facsimile on CD-ROM (2004), with images from the manuscript and commentary (in French, English, and German).

We offer several images from this beautiful manuscript. One copy of the facsimile is open at Pl. 3 (f. 2v), the Calendar page for February. In the foreground is a farm, with a village (marked by the church steeple) visible at a distance. The farmyard, even in February and despite the apparent chill, is full of life: we can see a dovecote, beehives, and a full sheepfold. The wall of the farmhouse has been cut away to give us a peek at the farm wife (in blue) and two other women warming their legs (somewhat indecently) by the fire.

A second image from the Calendar, that for the month of May (Pl. 6; f. 5v), can be seen on the facsimile's slipcase. Here, the Duc de Berry and his court have gone a'maying, riding in the woods behind a group of musicians: some of the ladies wear green, some have garlands in their hair, as is appropriate to May Day. The roofs in the distance appear to be the city of Paris.

The second copy of the facsimile is open to the Plan of the City of Rome (Pl. 106; f. 141v). Rome is represented here primarily in terms of the sites of greatest interest to travellers and pilgrims, both the classical remains as well as churches that house important relics. In the lower right, for instance, across the Tiber from the main portion of the city, is the Vatican, the centre of Christendom for medieval Europeans and one of the principal destinations for pilgrims. ✲

Les très riches heures du duc de Berry et l'enluminure en France au début du XVe siècle: Exposition au Musée Condé du 31 mars au 2 août 2004. Paris: Somogy; Chantilly: Musée Condé, 2004.

41. The Book of the Knight Zifar

Manuscript: Paris, Bibliothèque nationale de France, Ms. espagnol 36.

Produced in Castille, sometime in the fifteenth century (greater precision is not currently possible).

Paper, with the first leaf of parchment; 192 leaves; 41.5 x 27.2 cm.

Decorated, and includes 242 miniatures illustrating the story.

Script: Gothic cursive.

Facsimile on display: *Libro del Caballero Zifar, códice de Paris*. 2 vols. Barcelona: M. Moleiro Editor, 1996.

THE *Libro del Caballero Zifar* is a Spanish-language chivalric romance, composed in the early fourteenth century, that tells a leisurely story of Sir Zifar's journey, accompanied by his wife, Grima, and their two sons, as they travel westward from India to seek Europe, a land of Christian hope and promise. It became quite popular when first printed in Seville in 1512, and it is possible that Cervantes was influenced by it when he wrote *Don Quixote*. The Paris manuscript, seen here, is one of two medieval copies of the work, the other being preserved in Madrid.

Some 250 images related to this manuscript are reproduced in the Bibliothèque nationale's "Mandragore" image database, <http://mandragore.bnf.fr/>.

In one of the miniatures in the opening on display (ff. 32v–33r) we see a lioness carrying away Garfin, Zifar's elder son, just outside the city of Falac (Book I, Chap. 39); on the facing page, we see the city of Falac, with several men on the ramparts. ✻

Libro del Cauallero Çifar. Ed. Marilyn A. Olsen. Spanish Series 16. Madison: Hispanic Seminary of Medieval Studies, 1984.

42. John Lydgate. *The Lives of Ss. Edmund and Fremund*

Manuscript: London, British Library, MS Harley 2278.
Produced probably in Bury St. Edmunds (or, possibly, London), ca. 1434.
Fine vellum; 119 leaves; 24.8 x 17.5 cm.
Decorated and illuminated; 120 miniatures (2 full-page).
Script: Gothic semi-cursive.
Facsimile on display: *The Life of St Edmund, King and Martyr: The Lives of Saints Edmund and Fremund in MS Harley 2278*. Ed. A.S.G. Edwards. 2 vols. London: Folio Society, 2004.

After his second coronation, in Paris, King Henry VI (then a boy of twelve) and his court "retired" for a time to the monastery of Bury St. Edmunds in East Anglia (Christmas 1433 through Easter 1434). At the command of Abbot Curteys, and as a gift from the abbey to the king in commemoration of the royal visit, John Lydgate, a monk of the abbey and already a poet with royal favour, produced an English poetic life of the patron saint of the abbey, Edmund, king of East Anglia, and martyr (killed by Vikings in 869). Lydgate turned this into a "double life" by including as well the life of St. Fremund, supposedly Edmund's Warwickshire nephew, whose success against the Vikings was explained as God's vengeance for their killing of Edmund. Lydgate's poem was copied, decorated, and illustrated in a deluxe manuscript, which may well have been produced in the abbey's scriptorium or in a commercial scriptorium associated with the abbey. This is almost certainly the manuscript presented to the king; it is a "royal" manuscript in terms of the quality of its production and lavish illustration, and it is the earliest known manuscript produced in England to include an extensive set of illustrations to a story; there is, on average, one miniature per opening.

The opening on display here (ff. 27v–28r) includes two miniatures. On the left, Edmund (who, according to the legend, was born and raised in Saxony, and came from there to East Anglia to claim his crown) and his companions arrive in England, landing at St. Edmund's Point. On the right, Edmund prays for water, and springs appear miraculously. Edmund and his companions, according to the story, built on this site the town of Hunstanton (now "Old Hunstanton" to distinguish the medieval village from the adjacent Victorian seaside resort of Hunstanton), and the miraculous spring can still be seen by the village church. ✻

Scott, Kathleen L. *Later Gothic Manuscripts, 1390–1490*. 2 vols. A Survey of Manuscripts Illuminated in the British Isles 6. London: Harvey Miller Publishers, 1996. 1: 225–29 (Item 78) and Ills. 310–13.

Seymour, M.C. "Some Lydgate Manuscripts: *Lives of SS Edmund and Fremund* and *Danse Macabre*." *Edinburgh Bibliographical Society Transactions* 5.4 (1983–1984, 1984–1985): 10–24.

43. The Hours of Catherine of Cleves

Manuscripts: New York, Pierpont Morgan Library, MS M.917 and M.945.
Produced in Utrecht, ca. 1440.
M.917: Parchment; 164 leaves; 19.2 x 13.0 cm.
Decorated and illuminated; 94 miniatures (10 full-page).
Script: Gothic bookhand ("black letter"; "littera textualis formata").
M.945: Parchment; 194 leaves; 19.2 x 13.0 cm.
Decorated and illuminated; 1 historiated initial; 63 miniatures (15 full-page).
Facsimile on display: *The Hours of Catherine of Cleves*. Ed. John Plummer. New York: George Braziller, 1966.

This beautiful Book of Hours was split into several parts in the 1850s, probably by an unscrupulous bookseller seeking to increase his profits; two substantial portions of the work are now owned by the Pierpont Morgan Library, but it is thought that at least ten miniatures are still missing. The book was produced in the mid-fifteenth century for Catherine of Cleves, Duchess of Guelders (d. 1476). The artist, known as the "Master of Catherine of Cleves," has also been identified as the principal artist in some thirteen other manuscripts produced in Utrecht during the period 1430–1460.

The facsimile is open to a miniature showing the "Holy Family at Work" (Pl. 92). This is a scene of medieval domestic tranquility and "cottage industry": Mother Mary sits, weaving at a loom, while Joseph the carpenter planes a board, and both keep one eye on the infant Jesus in his walker. The domestic goods are carefully depicted behind them: a shelf of silver or pewter plate, a cabinet of weaving materials, a fireplace with an adjustable hook for the cooking pot, and a carpenter's bench and tools. The child holds a banderole reading, in Latin, "I am your solace."

A second image is seen on the slipcase (reproducing Pl. 1), being a Madonna and Child with Catherine of Cleves kneeling in worship. The banderole issuing from her reads "O mater dei memento mei" ("O Mother of God, remember me"). The baby Jesus holds a pen which he is dipping into an inkwell held by his mother, presumably to make a record of Catherine's act of devotion. The border includes coats of arms of Catherine of Cleves and her ancestors. ❋

Defoer, Henri L.M., Anne S. Korteweg, and Wilhelmina C.M. Wüstefeld. *The Golden Age of Dutch Manuscript Painting*. Intro. James H. Marrow. New York: George Braziller, 1990. 152–57 (Items 45–46); cf. 146–50 on "The Master of Catherine of Cleves, ca. 1430–1460."

44. The Black Hours of Galeazzo Maria Sforza

Manuscript: Vienna, Österreichische Nationalbibliothek, Cod. Vindobonensis 1856.
Produced in Bruges, ca. 1451–1475.
Fine vellum (tinted black); 154 leaves; ca. 25.0 x 17.5 cm.
Decorated and illuminated; 10 historiated initials; 15 full-page miniatures; 24 Calendar miniatures; 71 roundels. Text in silver and gold.
Script: Gothic bookhand ("black letter"; "littera textualis formata").
Artist: The Master of the Black Prayer books (Philippe de Mazerolles?).
Facsimile on display: *Manuscrit 1856: Le livre d'heures noir du duc Galeazzo Maria Sforza: miniatures éditées et commentée par O. Smital; volume de fac-similé avec 61 planches en couleurs et 15 photogravures dans le volume de texte*. Ed. O. Smital. Vienna: Edition de l'Impr. d'Etat autrichienne, 1930.

This is another "Psalter-Hours," a Book of Hours accompanied by a complete Psalter, and is of a most unusual and very striking appearance, with silver and gold text on black-tinted vellum. It is thought that the book was originally commissioned by Charles the Bold, Duke of Burgundy, but it quickly passed from him to Galeazzo Maria Sforza, the Duke of Milan.

The facsimile is opened to the first page of the Mass of the Virgin Mary (ff. 27v–28r). On the left is an image of a chapel, upon the altar of which is a statue of the Madonna and Child, before which various worshippers are kneeling. ❋

Pächt, Otto, and Dagmar Thoss. *Flämische Schule II*. 2 vols. Veröffentlichungen der Kommission für Schrift- und Buchwesen des Mittelalters, Reihe I: Die Illuminierten Handschriften und Inkunabeln der Österreichischen Nationalbibliothek Bd. 7. Vienna: Verlag der Österreichischen Akademie der Wissenschaften, 1990. I: 17–35, with Abb. 12–41 and Figs. 3–18.

45. King René's Book of Love *(Le livre du cueur d'amours espris)*

Manuscript: Vienna, Österreichische Nationalbibliothek, Cod. Vindobonensis 2597.
Produced in Anjou, ca. 1468.
Parchment; 127 leaves; 29.0 x 20.7 cm.
Luxuriously decorated and illuminated; 16 miniatures (with spaces reserved for another 29, not completed).
Script: Gothic cursive.
Artist: "the *Cueur* Master" (Barthélemy de Eyck?).
Facsimiles on display:
1) *Le livre du cueur d'amours espris. The National Library, Vienna*. Ed. F. Unterkircher. Trans. Sophie Wilkins. London: Thames and Hudson, 1975.
2) *King René's Book of Love / Le cueur d'amours espris. The National Library, Vienna*. Ed. F. Unterkircher. Trans. Sophie Wilkins. New York: George Braziller, 1975.

Le livre du cueur d'amour espris is an elaborate love allegory (in the tradition of the *Roman de la Rose*), written by René, King of Naples and Sicily, and Duke of Anjou and Provence, around 1457. There are six manuscripts of the work; the Vienna manuscript is the oldest, completed about 1468 (the other five are of several decades later), and it is the most beautifully decorated.

The story tells how Sir Heart, accompanied by his page, Desire, is on a quest to find the loveliest of ladies, Sweet Grace; he has many adventures along the way, and overcomes many obstacles. The illustrations include elaborate and extensive landscapes, and show skill in the use of perspective, careful modelling, and a sense of three dimensionality, as well as subtlety in lighting effects (not least in the several pictures set at night, at dawn, and at dusk).

On the slipcase is reproduced f. 5v, where we see Sir Heart (in black armour) and Desire (dressed in white) speak with Lady Hope, who promises to support all true lovers on their quests, in fulfillment of the commandment given to her by the god Amour. Amour's commandment is printed on the pillar beside which she stands.

One copy of the facsimile is open to f. 9r, where Sir Heart emerges from the forest and comes upon a chapel or hermitage, where they are met by the very personification of ugliness. She is Jealousy, who has captured and imprisoned Fair Welcome, whom the god Amour had sent to greet the travellers. In response to their request for directions to the Castle of Good Rest, Jealousy sends them off in the wrong direction, into the Forest of Long Waiting.

The second copy shows f. 18v (also reproduced on the cover of this catalogue): Dame Melancholy, the friend of no man, has led Sir Heart and Desire along the Stream of Tears, until they come to the Bridge Perilous, so narrow that only one may cross at a time, and so weak that it could crumble at any moment. The bridge is guarded by a knight in black named Anxiety, who prevents any lover from crossing. Sir Heart and Sir Anxiety are in the process of couching their lances and preparing to joust on the bridge. ✲

René I, King of Naples and Jerusalem. *The Book of the Love-Smitten Heart*. Ed. and trans. Stephanie Viereck Gibbs and Kathryn Karczewska. New York: Routledge, 2001.

——. *Le coeur d'amour epris: Reproduction intégrale en fac-similé des miniatures du Codex Vindobonensis 2597 de la Bibliothèque nationale de Vienne*. Ed. Marie-Thérèse Gousset, Daniel Poirion, and Franz Unterkircher. Paris: Philippe Lebaud, 1981.

46. The Book of Hours of Mary of Burgundy

Manuscript: Vienna, Österreichische Nationalbibliothek, Cod. Vindobonensis 1857.
Produced in Flanders; 1478 or 1479.
Parchment; 186 leaves; 22.5 x 16.3 cm.
Decorated and illuminated; 14 historiated initials; 62 miniatures (20 full-page).
Script: Gothic bookhand ("black letter"; "littera textualis formata").
Artist: The "Master of Mary of Burgundy" (possibly Nicholas Spierinc; possibly Alexander Bening).
Facsimile on display: *Gebetbuch Karls des Kühnen; vel potius, Stundenbuch der Maria von Burgund: Codex Vindobonensis 1857 der Österreichischen Nationalbibliothek*. Ed. Franz Unterkircher and Antoine de Schryver. 2 vols. Codices selecti phototypice impressi 14. Graz: Akademische Druck- u. Verlagsanstalt, 1969.

THIS is a very attractive Book of Hours, once thought to have been owned by Charles the Bold, Duke of Burgundy, but now thought to have been owned by his daughter Mary (1457–1482), the wife of Maximilian I of the House of Hapsburg (the future Archduke of Austria and Holy Roman Emperor). The identity of the artist, the "Master of Mary of Burgundy" (responsible for both this Book of Hours as well as the next item in the exhibition), has been the subject of much speculation, but Alexander Bening and Nicholas Spierinc, both of whom are associated with a number of similar books, are the two artists most frequently proposed.

Ff. 14v–15r, the opening shown here, includes a quite lovely and complex miniature: in the foreground, a lady (Mary of Burgundy, presumably) is seen with her dog in her lap and with an open prayer book (perhaps this Book of Hours). The table holds jewels and flowers, and there is some rich cloth in a heap below. The glazed window opens into a second interior space, with the appearance of a Gothic cathedral, where we see an altar, in front of which are seated the Virgin and Child, various worshippers before them, and several putti leaning against candlesticks. On the facing page, in the historiated initial, we see an image of the Vision of Thomas of Canterbury concerning the Seven Joys of the Virgin. ✻

Pächt, Otto. *The Master of Mary of Burgundy*. London: Faber and Faber, 1948. 64–65 (Item 7) and Pls. 10–13, 19, 40(b), 40(c), and 45.

———, and Dagmar Thoss. *Flämische Schule II*. 2 vols. Veröffentlichungen der Kommission für Schrift- und Buchwesen des Mittelalters, Reihe 1: Die Illuminierten Handschriften und Inkunabeln der Österreichischen Nationalbibliothek Bd. 7. Vienna: Verlag der Österreichischen Akademie der Wissenschaften, 1990. 1: 69–85, with Farbtafel X, Abb. 102–50, and Figs. 55–75.

47. The Hours of Engelbert of Nassau

Manuscript: Oxford, Bodleian Library, MSS Douce 219 and 220.

Produced in Flanders, ca. 1480–1490.

Parchment; 159 + 127 leaves; 14.2 x 10.6 cm.

Decorated and illuminated; historiated initials; 62 miniatures.

Script: Gothic bookhand ("black letter"; "littera textualis formata").

Artist: The "Master of Mary of Burgundy" (possibly Nicholas Spierinc; possibly Alexander Bening).

Facsimile on display: *A Book of Hours for Engelbert of Nassau, the Bodleian Library, Oxford*. Ed. J.J.G. Alexander. New York: George Braziller, 1970.

THIS BOOK OF HOURS was originally produced for Engelbert of Nassau (Engelbrecht II, Count of Nassau-Dillenberg-Dietz, 1451–1504), Lieutenant of the Realm under Philip the Fair (b. 1478; the son of Mary of Burgundy and Maximilian I of the House of Hapsburg). It seems, however, to have passed quickly into the possession of Philip the Fair, whose arms occur seven times in the manuscript, usually painted over the arms of Engelbert. This revision was not carried to completion, however, for there are still several pages decorated with peacock feathers, one of Engelbert's devices, and Engelbert's motto appears in the lower border of f. 214r.

We display here Pls. 75–76 (ff. 114v–115r), the beginning of Lauds in the Hours of the Virgin. The miniature on the left represents the Visitation: in a summer setting, an aging Elizabeth kneels before a very young Mary and kisses her hand. Facing this, in contrast to that summer scene, is a winter scene of the Nativity, showing Joseph and Mary in a very medieval and northern European "Bethlehem," as Joseph and Mary are denied a room at the inn. The border is solid gold over-painted with flowers and leaves, and there is a lovely butterfly on the left edge. ✲

Pächt, Otto. *The Master of Mary of Burgundy*. London: Faber and Faber, 1948. 67 (Item 14) and Col. Pls. A-D and Pls. 16, 20, 21, 28, 30–34, 37, 38(b), 41(b), 43, and 48.

——, and J.J.G. Alexander. *Illuminated Manuscripts in the Bodleian Library, Oxford*. 3 vols. Oxford: Clarendon Press, 1966–1973. 1: 27 (Item 361).

48. A Book of Hours by Jean Bourdichon

Manuscript: Vatican City, Biblioteca Apostolica Vaticana, Cod. Vat. lat. 3781.

Produced in Tours, ca. 1485.

Parchment; 118 leaves; 15.8 x 9.8 cm.

Decorated and illuminated; many ornate capitals; 17 miniatures.

Script: Gothic semi-cursive.

Artist: Jean Bourdichon.

Facsimile on display: *Vat. lat. 3781: Offizium der Madonna (Ms. Vat. lat. 3781): Entstanden Ende des 15. Jahrhunderts.* 2 vols. Codices e Vaticanis selecti 67. Zurich: Belser Verlag, 1984.

JEAN BOURDICHON (1457?–1521?), court painter to four kings of France, was an artist and designer, associated with stained glass windows, engravings, coin designs, and easel paintings, as well as manuscript illuminations. He was responsible for two of the items in this exhibition, this Book of Hours (for an unknown patron) and the Book of Hours of Anne de Bretagne (Item 54).

The opening on display (ff. 30v–31r) is another representation of the Visitation of Mary to Elizabeth (the usual subject for an image at the beginning of the text of Lauds of the Hours of the Blessed Virgin). An older Elizabeth kneels before the young Mary, with an expansive landscape, including a house on a hill, behind them. Around the miniature is a floral border, including a bird among the flowers on the left edge, and a centaur at the bottom. ✻

49. The Schedel World Map

Printed in 1493 in Nuremberg.
Paper, printed from woodcuts.
Facsimile on display: new edition printed from an original woodcut by Zsolt Török.

THE SCHEDEL WORLD MAP appeared in 1493 in the first edition of a history of the world, or *Liber chronicarum*, that was published in Nuremberg. The work, which was compiled and printed by Hartmann Schedel (1440–1514), is also commonly known as *The Nuremberg Chronicle*, and it was reprinted many times after 1493. It has been suggested that a young Albrecht Dürer (1471–1528) may even have been involved in the project. The *Chronicle* is an illustrated history of the world, and divides the ages of man into six, with a seventh age encompassing the final judgement.

The map on display is a Ptolemaic world map, and it depicts the three sons of Noah holding its edges, as the story of the flood in Genesis 6–9 was commonly believed to have resulted in the settling of different areas of the world by different sons: Sem settled Asia, Japhet settled Europe, and Cham settled Africa. The panel on the left is an adaptation of the original edition of the *Chronicle*, and it was added by the creator of the new edition to distinguish it from the original. The panel depicts several of the monstrous races commonly associated with medieval cartography and "Wonders of the East" tradition.

More information on this, and the other items by Professor Török (Items 51, 59, and 62), is available on his website: <http://lazarus.elte.hu/~zoltorok/Cartartweb/cartart_maps.htm>. ✻

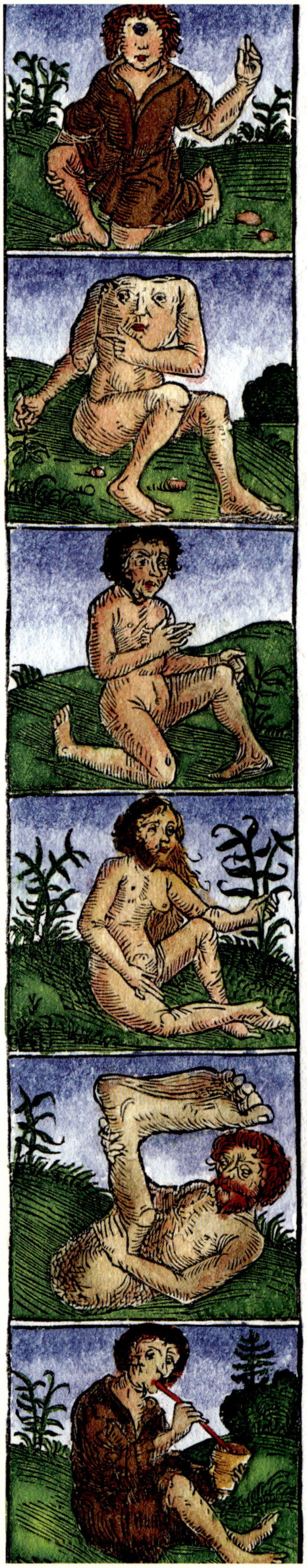

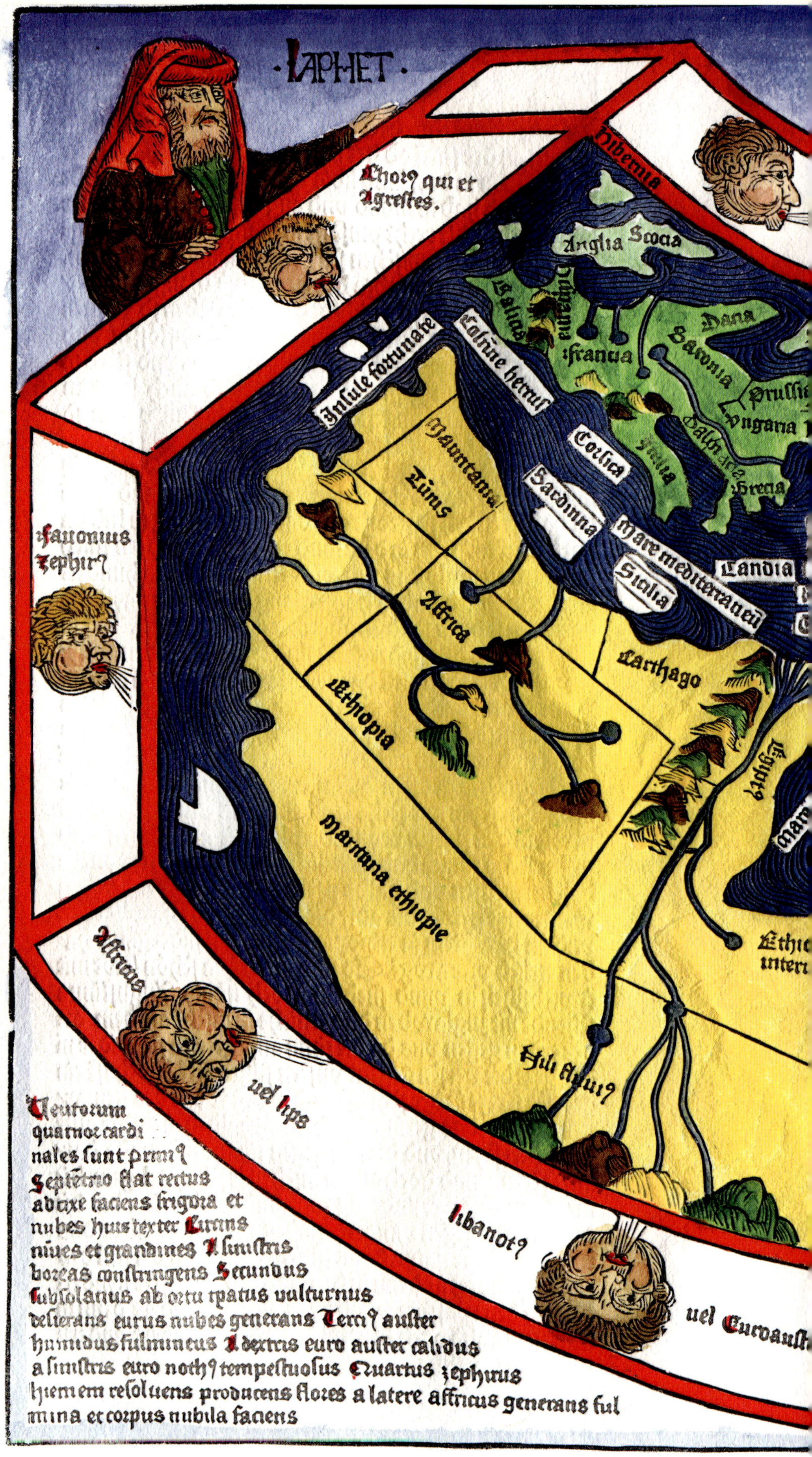

IAPHET
Chorus qui et Agrestes.
Hibernia
Anglia Scocia
Insule fortunate
Colüne herculis
Francia
Saxonia
Dacia
Prussia
Ungaria
Gallia
Ytalia
Grecia
Corsica
Sardinia
Mauritania
Tinus
Mare mediterraneum
Sicilia
Landia
Affrica
Carthago
Ethiopia
Egiptus
Maritima ethiopie
Fauonius Zephirus
Affricus
uel lips
Nili fluuius
libanotus
uel Euroauster
Uentorum quattuor cardinales sunt primus Septētrio flat rectus ab axe faciens frigora et nubes huius texter Circius a dextris niues et grandines A sinistris boreas constringens Secundus subsolanus ab ortu spatius vulturnus desierans eurus nubes generans Tercius auster humidus fulmineus A dextris euro auster calidus a sinistris euro nothus tempestuosus Quartus zephirus hiemem resoluens producens flores a latere affricus generans fulmina et corpus nubila faciens

Fig. 18

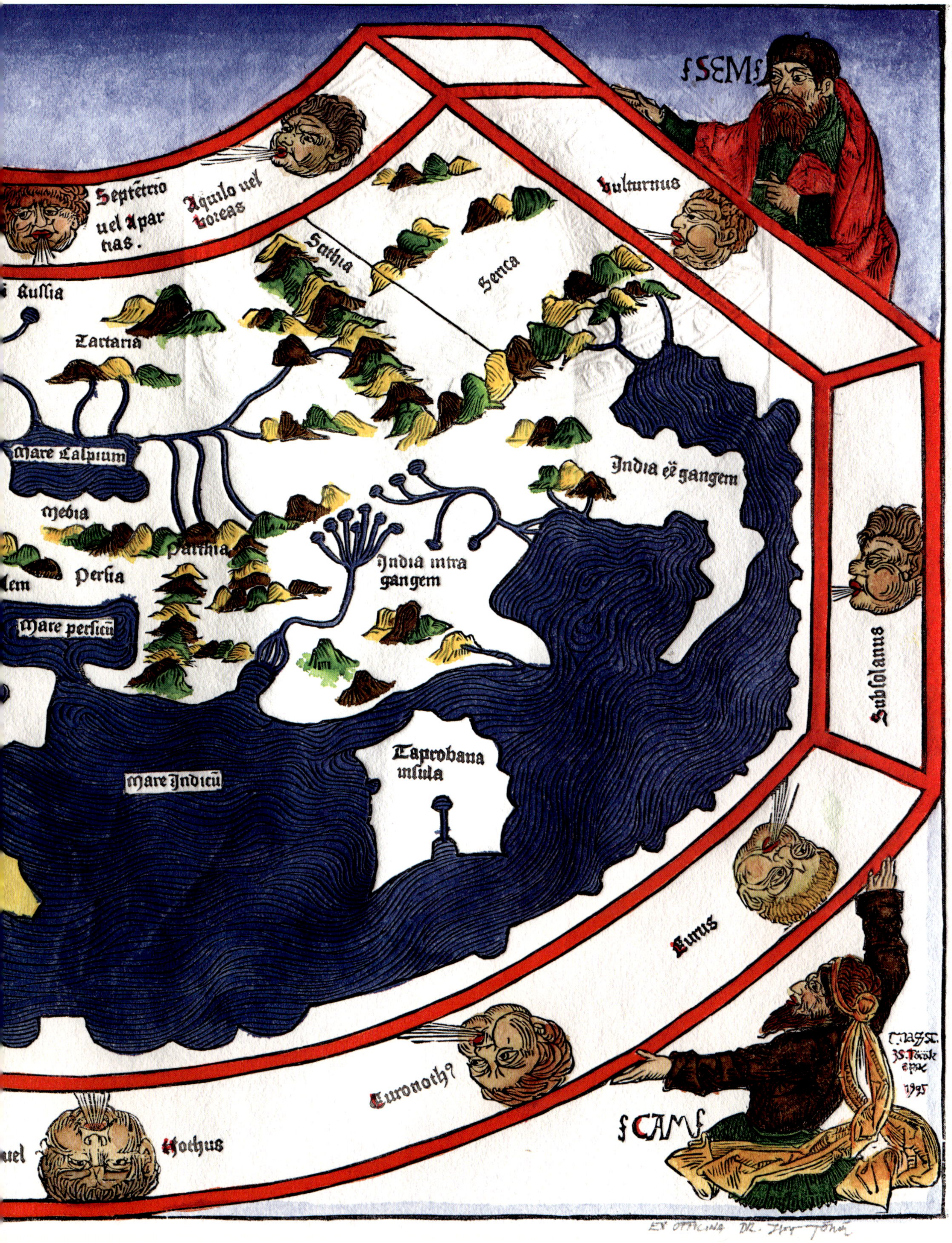
SEM
Septētrio uel Apar nas.
Aquilo uel boreas
Vulturnus
Scithia
Serica
Russia
Tartaria
Mare Caspium
India extra gangem
Media
Parthia
Persia
India intra gangem
Mare persicu
Mare Indicu
Taprobana insula
Subsolanus
Eurus
Euronoth?
Nothus
CAM
1995

50. The Sea Chart of Judah Abenzara

Manuscript: Vatican City, Biblioteca Apostolica Vaticana, Cod. Borgiano VII.
Produced in Alexandria, 1497.
Parchment; 1 roll; 67 x 106 cm.
Facsimile on display: *Seekarte des Iehuda ben Zara (Borgiano VII 1497)*. Ed. Arthur Dürst. Codices e Vaticanis selecti 55. Zurich: Belser Verlag, 1983.

ABOUT JUDAH ABENZARA (also often known as Iehuda ben Zara and Jehuda ben Zara and with many other variations on the name and in capitalization) very little is known. He seems to have been a mapmaker working in Alexandria, active at least between 1490 and 1505. Three of his maps survive, and the "Seekarte" (a "portolan" map, intended primarily to show seaports for the use of mariners) from the Vatican Library is the earliest of the three. The map is considered to be one of the finest maps of the Vatican's collection. The reproduction is exactly to scale and weight, and includes all six of the colours and the gold leaf of the original. As the absence of sewing indicates, the map was drawn on the full skin of one animal. It represents the latest knowledge of the known world in 1497. ✻

Roth, Cecil, "Judah Abenzara's Map of the Mediterranean World, 1500." *Studies in Bibliography and Booklore* 9.2–3 (Spring 1970): 116–20.

51. The Romweg Map

Produced in Nuremberg, ca. 1500.
Paper, broadsheet, printed from woodblock by the publisher Jörg Glockendon; 41 x 29 cm.
Facsimile on display: new edition printed from original woodcut by Zsolt Török.

THE ROMWEG MAP was produced by Erhard Etzlaub (1455?–1532), a physician, cartographer, and instrument maker who spent the majority of his life in Nuremberg. The map's title means "Rome-way": the map was intended to guide pilgrims on their journey to Rome in the spiritually significant year 1500. It is the earliest printed map and road map of central Europe.

The map itself orients south at the top, and dotted lines are used to indicate major routes for pilgrimage. Each dot, in fact, also represents a "German Mile," or approximately 7.4 kilometres. Apparently the map was designed to be used with a sun compass, an example of which is drawn at the bottom of the map.

52. Pierre Sala's Little Book of Love (*Le petit livre d'amour*)

Manuscript: London, British Library, MS Stowe 955.
Produced in Paris, ca. 1500.
Fine vellum (tinted purple), with letters in gold or in red; 21 leaves; 13.0 x 10.0 cm.
Decorated and illuminated; 12 full-page miniatures.
Script: Gothic cursive.
Artist: "Master of the Chronique Scandaleuse."
Facsimile on display: Sala, Pierre. *Petit livre d'amour: Stowe MS 955, British Library, London.* Ed. Janet Backhouse and Yves Giraud. 2 vols. Lucerne: Faksimile Verlag, 1994.

This is a charming little book, created by Pierre Sala (Master of the Horse in the court of King Charles VIII) as a gift for his lady, Marguerite Builloud, in an attempt (successful) to persuade her to marry him. Each miniature, enclosed inside a frame of gold penwork, is an emblematic representation of an idea about love, and the short poetic text on the facing page helps to confirm the idea. The text pages are decorated with repeated "P" and "M" monograms, presumably for "Pierre" and "Marguerite," as well as a repeated device that might be a crossing of a pair of compasses. The book is prefaced with a four-page address from Sala to his lady, and the final miniature in the sequence is a very realistic portrait of him.

The book was enclosed in an elaborately carved wooden box covered in leather, decorated again with "P" and "M" monograms. It was designed to protect the book and to permit it to be hung from the lady's belt, should she desire to keep it with her. The publishers of the facsimile have included with it a replica of this container.

The book is open to an image showing a group of young people in a garden of red and white flowers. A young lover has been blindfolded. Although another lady taps him on the shoulder in an attempt to distract him, nevertheless he reaches for his lady: although his eyes are blind, his heart is unerringly drawn to her. The text on the facing page reads

Sune foys jen puys tenyr vne
e[lle] ne meschappera de lan
et me deust lon donner myllan
Londres parys et pampelune

["If ever I manage to catch a lady,
I will never let her go, were I offered
Milan, London, Paris, and Pampluna
in exchange."] ✲

53. The Rosary of Joan the Mad

Manuscript: fragments only; sixteen dispersed leaves identified to date:
Cambridge, Fitzwilliam Museum, MS 257a and 257b (two leaves);
Boston, Boston Public Library, MS Med. 35 (twelve leaves);
Boston, Boston Public Library, Acc. no. 82–157 (two leaves).
Produced in Flanders, ca. 1500.
Fine vellum; 16 separate leaves; ca. 10.0 x 8.0 cm.
Decorated and illuminated; 16 miniatures.
Script: Gothic cursive.
Artist: Simon Bening or an associate (Bening's name is also associated with the Grimani Breviary [Item 55], and many other manuscripts).
Facsimile on display: *Rosario de Juana la Loca*. 2 vols. Valencia: Patrimonio Ediciones, 2004.

THIS is an example of a "rosary," which is a form of personal prayer book even simpler than a Book of Hours. While saying a set number of the prayers "Hail Mary," "Our Father," and the "Gloria" (using the rosary beads — a set of which accompany this facsimile — to help one to keep accurate count), one would contemplate, aided by pictures in the book, scenes from the life of Christ, the life of the Virgin Mary, and so forth. The several preserved leaves of this particular rosary have full-page miniatures from the life of the Virgin; on the obverse of each is the text of a prayer, with decorative borders in gold along all four edges, with images of flowers, insects, and birds.

The Rosary is thought to have come from the workshop of Simon Bening (1483–1561), son of Alexander (who may have been responsible for the Book of Hours of Mary of Burgundy [Item 46] and may have helped to produce the Grimani Breviary [Item 55]). Simon's name is associated with many of the finest books made for members of the courts of Spain. The Rosary is associated with Juana, Queen of Castille (b. 1479; reigned 1504–1555), popularly known as "Juana la Loca" ("Joan the Mad"), since she is said to have been so passionately devoted to her husband that she went mad at his untimely death. She was married to Philip the Handsome, son of Maximilian I, the Archduke of Austria and the Holy Roman Emperor, and her son Charles was Holy Roman Emperor in his turn. (Her sister, Catherine of Aragon, was the first wife of Henry VIII of England, and the cause of his break with the Church of Rome.)

The opening on display shows ff. 2v–3r, including the scene of the Visitation of Mary to Elizabeth. There is a beautiful castle in the background, as well as a small windmill on the hill in the distance. Elizabeth kneels before Mary and places her hand on Mary's stomach. ✻

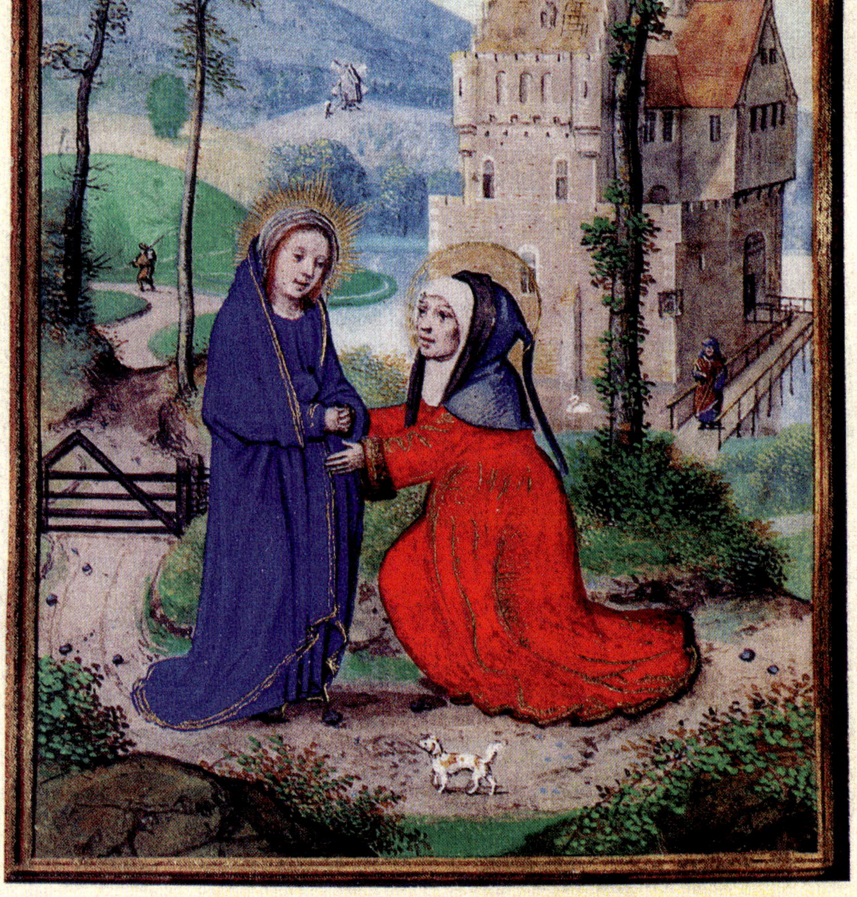

Fig. 19

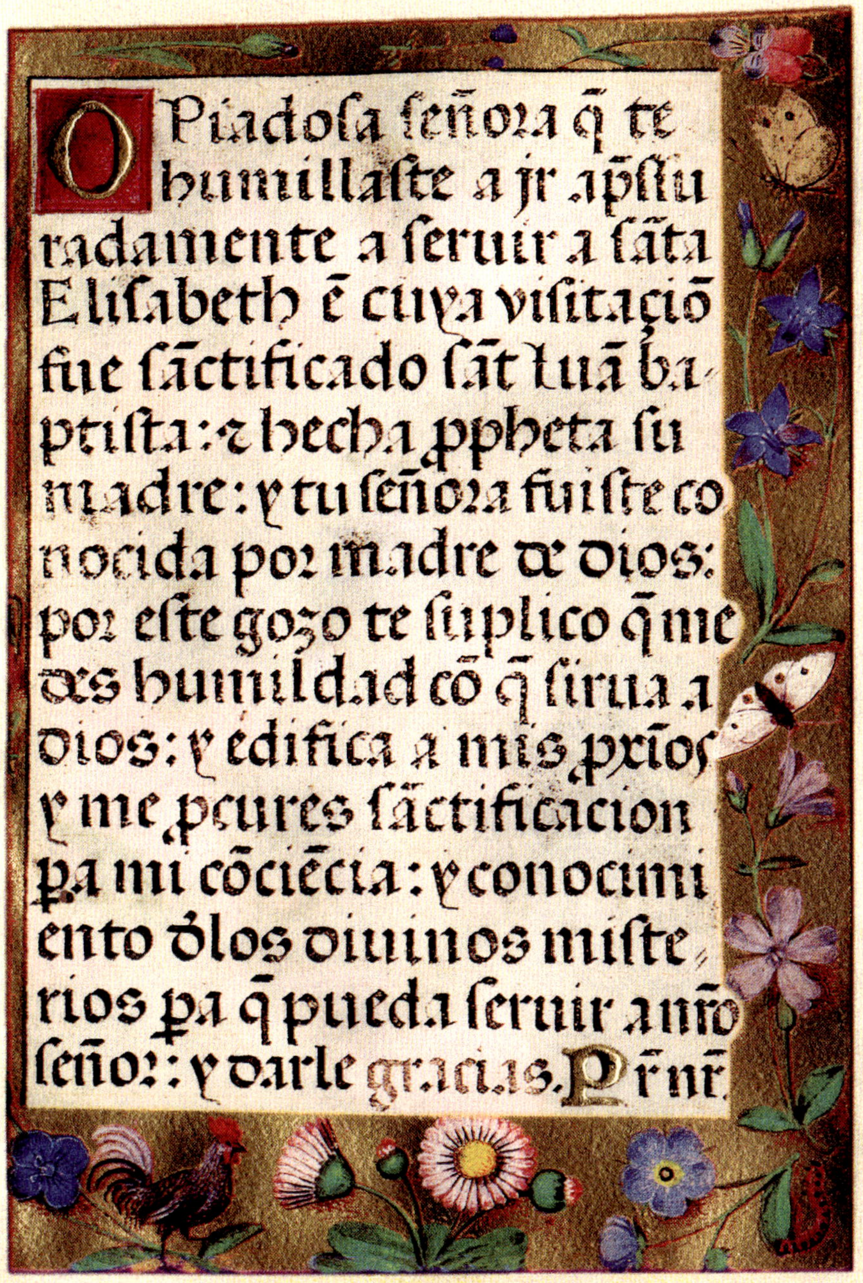
O Piadosa señora q̄ te
humillaste a jr apssu
radamente a seruir a sāta
Elisabeth ē cuya visitaciō
fue sātificado sāt Iuā ba
ptista: e hecha ppheta su
madre: y tu señora fuiste co
nocida por madre de dios:
por este gozo te suplico q̄ me
des humildad cō q̄ sirua a
dios: y edifica a mis pxios
y me pcures sāctificacion
pa mi cōciēcia: y conocimi
ento dlos diuinos miste
rios pa q̄ pueda seruir anr̄o
señor: y darle gracias. Pr̄ nr̄.

54. The Grandes Heures of Anne de Bretagne

Manuscript: Paris, Bibliothèque nationale de France, Ms. latin 9474.
Produced in Tours, ca. 1503–1508.
Parchment; 238 leaves; 30.5 x 20.0 cm.
Decorated and illuminated; 63 miniatures (49 full-page, each on black-tinted background).
Script: Gothic semi-cursive.
Artist: Jean Bourdichon (who also did the "Book of Hours by Jean Bourdichon" [Item 48], as well as many other manuscripts).
Facsimile on display: *Les heures d'Anne de Bretagne; Bibliothèque nationale (Manuscrit latin 9474)*. Intro. Émile Mâle. Captions by Edmond Pognon. *Verve* 14–15. Paris: Éditions Verve, 1946.

Anne de Bretagne (1477–1514) was Duchess of Brittany in her own right and one of the wealthiest women in Europe; she was twice an unwilling Queen of France, forced into marriage by military conquest, the king of France being determined to annex the Duchy of Brittany. Epics could be written of the wars she fought, the heroes she led, the defeat she suffered ("Of arms and unwelcome husbands I sing"). Her first marriage, to Maximilian I (Archduke of Austria, the future Holy Roman Emperor, whose first wife, Mary of Burgundy, had died in 1482), was conducted by proxy, never consummated, and was declared invalid by the Pope so that she could be compelled to marry her conqueror, King Charles VIII; after his death, by Charles' command, she was compelled to marry his cousin and heir, Louis XII (whose own first marriage had to be annulled by the Pope to free him to marry Anne in obedience to his cousin).

This Book of Hours is quite splendid, though the reproductions that we currently have do not do it justice. Besides the quality of the miniatures, the manuscript is also known for its floral decorations: there are some 330 different plants pictured in the margins, labelled with their Latin and French names, allowing this Book of Hours to double as a botanical encyclopedia. A colour facsimile of the full manuscript is in preparation, to be published by Moleiro in 2008. In the meantime, some 395 images from this manuscript are available in the Bibliothèque nationale's "Mandragore" image database, <http://mandragore.bnf.fr/>.

The image of the Visitation is displayed from the collection of reproductions published in *Verve* (Pl. IX). A second, and particularly striking image, partly for the way that it manages the light in a scene set at night (achieved, in part, by painting on black-tinted vellum), is that showing the arrest of Jesus, as Judas betrays Him to his enemies with a kiss.

Heures d'Anne de Bretagne: reproduction réduite des 63 peintures. Intro. Henri A. Omont. Paris: Berthaud, [1906].

Le livre d'heures d'Anne de Bretagne: manuscrit latin nò 9474 de la Bibliothèque nationale. Paris: Jean de Bonnot, 1979. (A complete, black-and-white facsimile, with commentaries on each miniature, including a full guide to the plant species represented, as well as a translation into French of the Latin text of the Book of Hours.)

Le livre d'heures de la reine Anne de Bretagne, traduit du latin et accompagné de notices inédites par M. l'abbé [Henri] Delaunay. 2 vols. Paris: L. Curmer, 1841. (Rpt. 1861.) (The second volume is a facsimile of the manuscript, with 50 chromolithographic plates and 345 text pages with coloured borders. This facsimile was produced in the days before photographic reproduction, so the engraving of each plate was done by hand.)

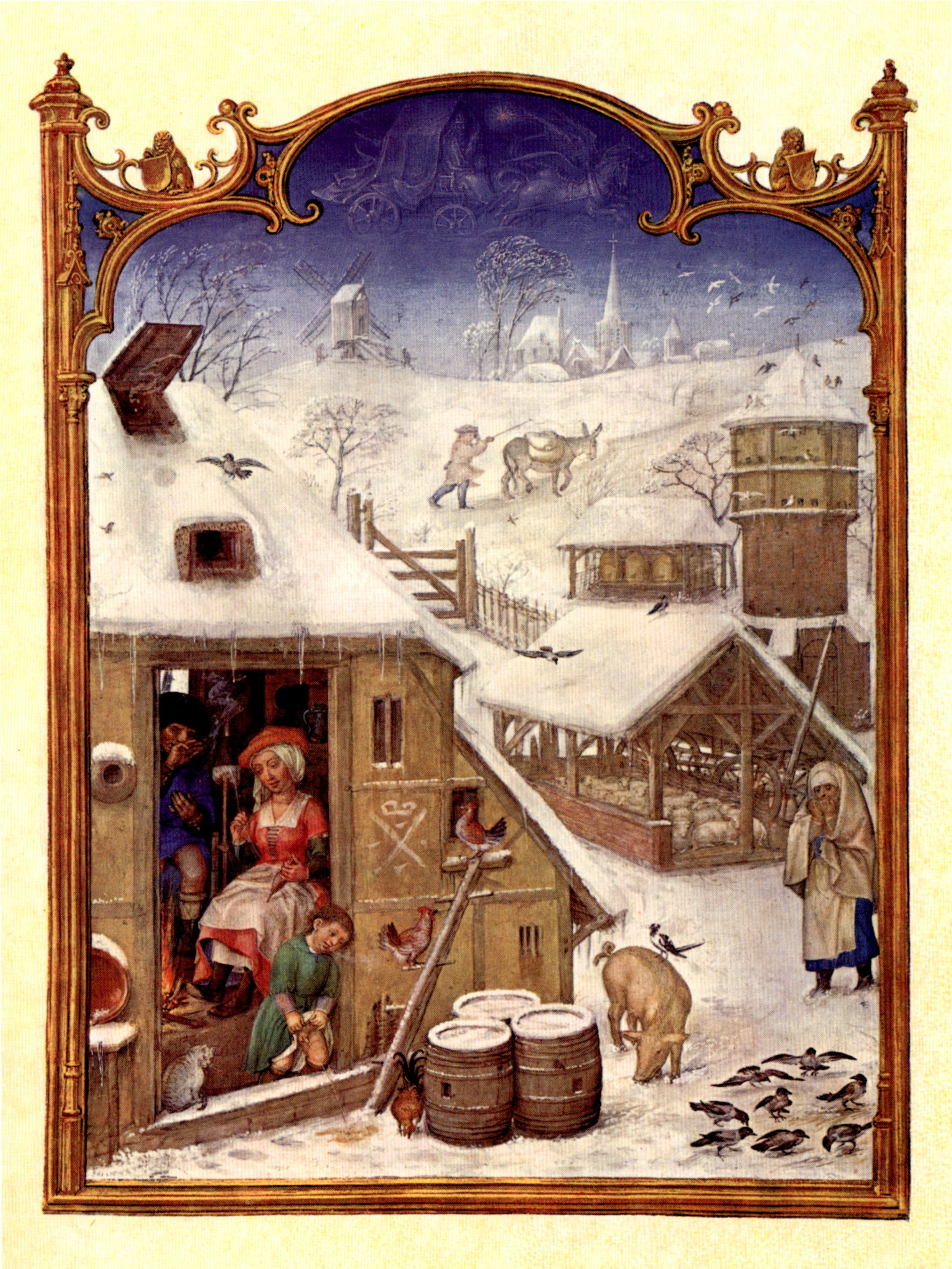

Fig. 20

55. The Grimani Breviary

Manuscript: Venice, Biblioteca Nazionale Marciana, MS Lat. XI 67 (7531).

Produced in Flanders, ca. 1500.

Fine vellum; 831 leaves; ca. 25.5 x 22.5 cm.

Decorated and illuminated; approx. 100 full-page miniatures, with many more smaller ones.

Artists: Gerard Horenbout (chief artist of the Calendar images in this manuscript, among others), Alexander Bening (who may also be the "Master of Mary of Burgundy"), and his son, Simon (who may have been responsible for the Rosary of Joan the Mad [Item 53]).

Facsimile on display: *The Grimani Breviary: Reproduced from the Illuminated Manuscript Belonging to the Biblioteca Marciana, Venice*. Intro. Mario Salmi. Pref. Georgio E. Ferrari. Trans. Simon Pleasance, Linda Packer, and Geoffrey Webb. London: Thames and Hudson, 1972.

A BREVIARY is another, and more formal, sort of prayer book, which gives the full text of the Divine Office (Liturgy of the Hours), including all of the variable "propers" for particular feast days. This is the sort of prayer book which would have been used by priests and monks, though it is not commonly found among the books of laypeople (for whom it may have seemed too complex for private devotions; the Book of Hours is a simpler variant of the Breviary, for lay use). This particular Breviary is said to have been commissioned for the Pope, but quickly passed into the possession of the Duke of Milan, from whom Cardinal Domenico Grimani of Venice acquired it about 1520. Through Antonio Grimani, the Doge of Venice, it passed to the city of Venice, and was deposited in the Library of St. Mark's Cathedral.

Flemish illuminators of the early sixteenth century imitated with some frequency the calendar pictures of the Très riches heures of Jean duc de Berry. The similarity between this version of the scene for "February" (Pl. 3, on display) and that of the Très riches heures is obvious, though the little boy purging himself in the doorway is new. (We are not the first to notice this particular innovation: Marcantonio Michiel saw the manuscript in 1521, soon after it had come into the possession of Cardinal Grimani, and he was quite effusive in his praise of the scenes for the twelve months, noting with delight "February, where a boy urinating in the snow turns it yellow and the surrounding countryside is frozen and covered in snow.") The editors of the facsimile suggest that the images of the Grimani Breviary reveal a desire for a heightened realism: "there is an attempt to portray the nuances of reality with a concrete quality which is quite removed from the exalted and ornate courtly depictions of the tangible world in the *Très Riches Heures* which belong to the fabulous world of the late Gothic period" (11). ✻

A Glance at the Grimani Breviary, Preserved in S. Mark's Library, Venice. Venice: F. Ongania, 1903.

56. The World Map of Bernardus Sylvanus

Produced in Venice in 1511.

Paper, printed woodcut: 41.2 x 49.7 cm.

Facsimile on display: *De universali habitabilis figura cum additionibus locorum nuper inventonum Venetiis MDXI / A Map of the Whole Habitable World with the Addition of Recently Discovered Places, Venice 1511.* Intro. David A. Woodward. Winnetka, IL: Speculum Orbis Press, 1983.

THE ITALIAN Bernardo Silvano (or Bernardus Sylvanus, as he is also called) produced this world map in 1511 for his edition of Ptolemy's *Geographia*, published in Venice by Giacomo Penzio. Silvano in fact produced two world maps for the edition, following Ptolemy closely in the first, and updating Ptolemy on the basis of modern discoveries for this, the final map of the edition. Almost nothing is otherwise known of Silvano.

The map is perhaps the first world map to be printed in two colours. Examples of Silvano's updating of Ptolemy include the "Terra laboratorus," "land of the labourer," or Labrador, and the "Regalis domus," "domain of the king," probably of Portugal. These two land masses had in previous world maps been attached to Asia, so it seems likely that Silvano was influenced by some early sixteenth-century Portuguese sources.

57. The Atlas Miller

Produced in Portugal, ca. 1519–1522.
Facsimile on display: *Atlas Miller*. Barcelona: M. Moliero Editor, 2003.

THE *Atlas Miller*, the original of which is currently in the Bibliothèque nationale de France, was produced by the cartographers Lopo Homem, Pedro Reinel, and Jorge Reinel, as well as the miniaturist António de Holanda. It has been suggested that the purpose of the *Atlas* might have been to subvert the idea that the mission being attempted by Ferdinand Magellan — the circumnavigation of the globe — was possible.

The panel on display depicts what Ptolemy's *Geographia* calls the *Magnus Sinus*, or the "Great Gulf," which is described on the map in the enclosed caption ("Hic est magnus golfus"): "This is the great gulf of the sea of the Chinese, in which there are large islands where they trade all manners of riches and merchandise." Students of geography might wonder what area of the world the map is intended to illustrate. It has been observed in the commentary volume that "this is perhaps the most beautiful chart in the entire Atlas Miller, yet it is simultaneously the falsest, and can categorically be labelled as somewhat fraudulent" (Miró 323). Where earlier maps of the "east" commonly included many beasts of the *Wonders* tradition (cf. Item 12), this chart includes only two, demonstrating one of the effects of the Renaissance upon cartography. ✻

Atlas Miller [commentary volume]. Ed. Mónica Miró. Barcelona: M. Moliero Editor, 2006.

58. The *Carta marina* of Olaus Magnus

Produced mainly in Rome between 1527 and 1539.
Paper, printed from woodcuts; 1.7 x 1.25 m. (in nine sheets).
Facsimile on display: *Olaus Magnus Carta marina 1539*. Ed. Herman Richter. Lychnos-bibliotek: Studier och källskrifter utgivna av Lärdomshistoriska samfundet 11.2. Lund: [Lychnos], 1967.

OLAUS MAGNUS' *Carta marina* (which simply means "Map of the Sea") is one of the earliest known maps of Scandinavia, and the earliest one to include details and place names. Olaus Magnus — who was himself a Swede, though he worked in Rome — later produced a *Historia de gentibus septentrionalibus* ("A History of the Northern Peoples"; 1555) which was, in essence, the full commentary to his earlier *Carta marina*.

The section of the map on display depicts Biarmia, also known as Bjarmaland or Permia, near modern-day Arkhangelsk in Russia, a region known since the time of the Old Norse sagas for strange and fantastic adventures. ✻

Lynam, Edward. *The Carta Marina of Olaus Magnus, Venice 1539 and Rome 1572*. Jenkintown, PA: Tall Tree Library, 1949.

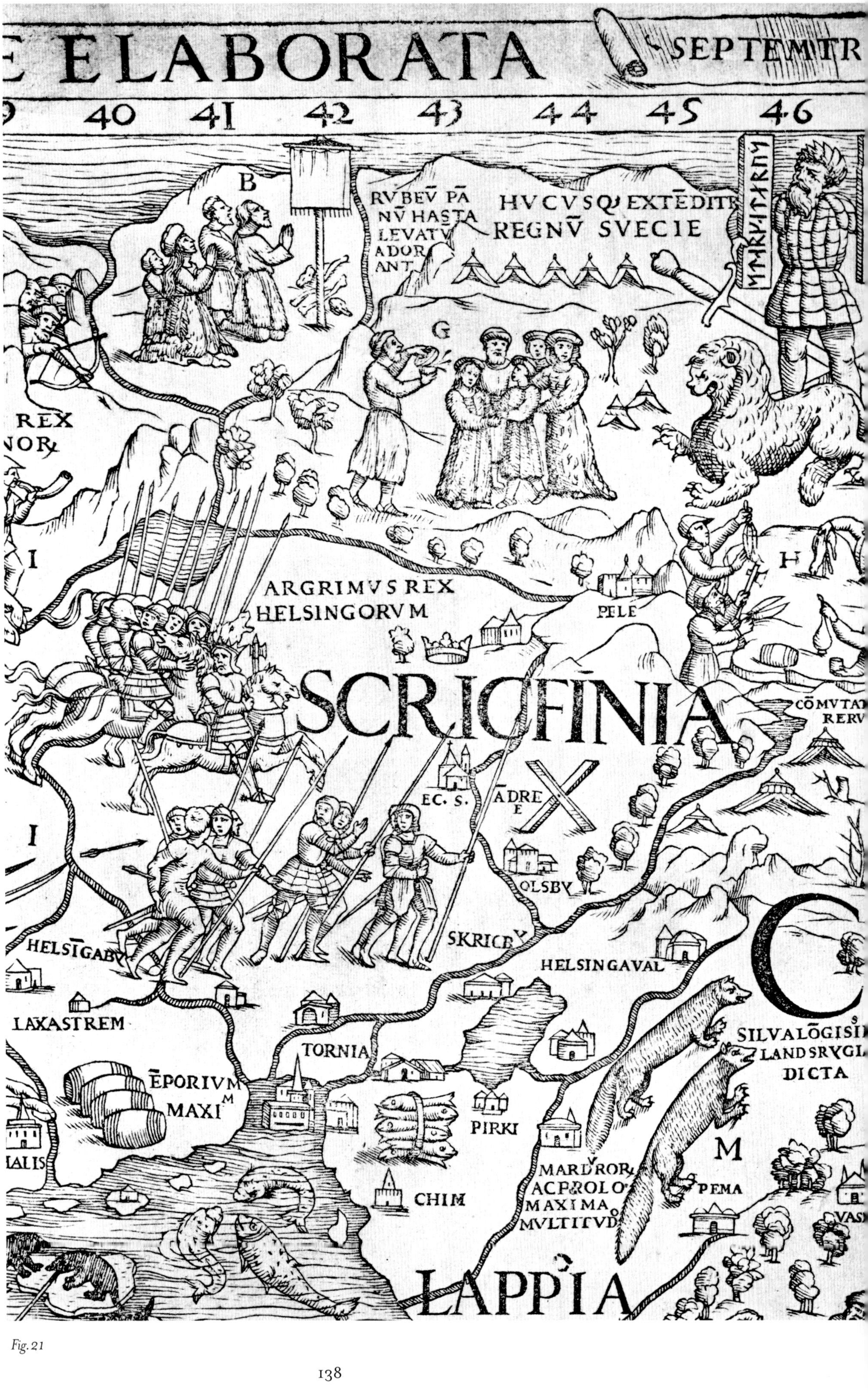
ELABORATA
SEPTEMTR
40 41 42 43 44 45 46
B
RVBEV PA
NV HASTA
LEVATV
ADOR
ANT
HVCVSQ EXTĒDITR
REGNV SVECIE
G
REX
NOR
I
ARGRIMVS REX
HELSINGORVM
PELE
H
SCRICFINIA
CŌMVTA
RERV
EC. S.
ADRE
E
I
OLSBY
SKRICE
HELSIGABY
HELSINGAVAL
LAXASTREM
TORNIA
SILVALŌGISI
LANDSRVGL
DICTA
ĒPORIVM
MAXIM
PIRKI
MARDVROR
ACP&OLO
MAXIMA
MVLTITVDO
M
PEMA
CHIM
LAPPIA

Fig. 21

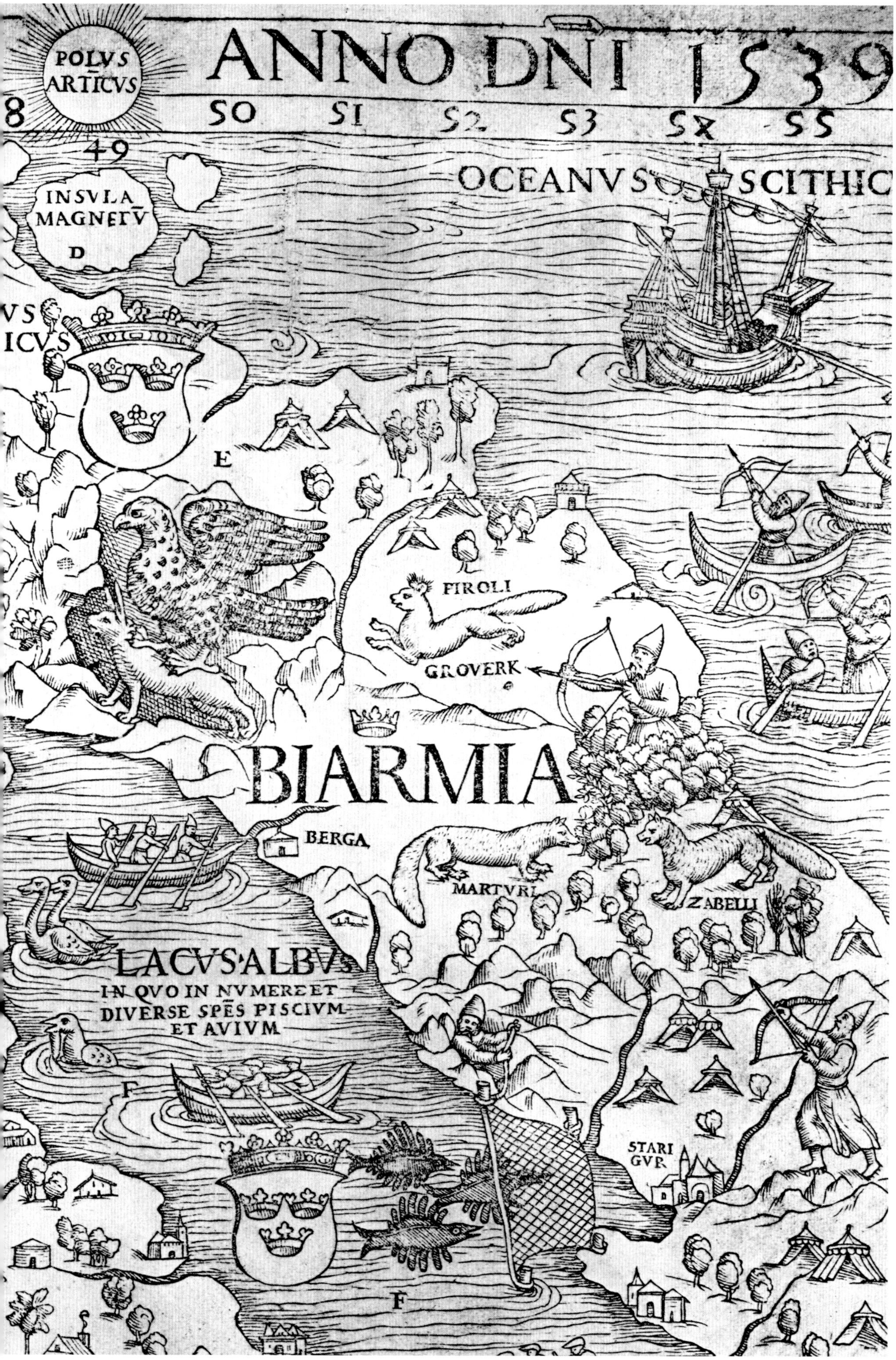
POLVS ARTICVS
ANNO DNI 1539
8
50 51 52 53 54 55
49
INSVLA MAGNETV
D
OCEANVS SCITHIC
VS
ICVS
E
FIROLI
GROVERK
BIARMIA
BERGA
MARTVRI
ZABELLI
LACVS ALBVS
IN QVO IN NVMERE ET DIVERSE SPES PISCIVM ET AVIVM
F
STARI GVR
F

59. The Münster Map of America

Produced in Basel in 1540.
Paper, printed from woodblock.
Facsimile on display: new edition printed from original woodcut by Zsolt Török.

THE MÜNSTER AMERICA was printed as part of Sebastian Münster's (1488–1552) edition of Ptolemy's *Geographia* (1540). It represents the first printed map dedicated to the depiction of the "New World" and was undoubtedly one of the most popular, as it was also featured in Münster's *Cosmographia*, which appeared in many editions, in many different languages, from its first edition in 1544 into the seventeenth century.

The creator of the new edition has suggested that the ship illustrated might have been intended to be that of Ferdinand Magellan. The map includes a "cannibal hut" and some "dismembered human body parts."

60. The Farnese Hours

Manuscript: New York, Pierpont Morgan Library, MS M.69.
Produced in Rome, 1546.
Fine vellum; 114 leaves; 17.3 x 11.0 cm.
Decorated initials and elaborate borders, with cameos, landscapes, and grotesques; includes 28 miniatures (three of which are double-page).
Script: Humanistic cursive (cancelleresca formata).
Artist: Giulio Clovio.
Facsimile on display: *The Farnese Hours, the Pierpont Morgan Library, New York*. Ed. Webster Smith. New York: George Braziller, [1976].

Completed in 1546, a century after Gutenberg's invention of movable type printing, this beautiful manuscript demonstrates that manuscript production did not end abruptly with the coming of the printed book, nor were the arts of the handmade book immediately forgotten. This Book of Hours was made for Cardinal Alessandro Farnese (1520–1589) by Giulio Clovio (1498–1578, a Croatian working in Rome, attached to the papal court). Clovio had been patronized for some time by Cardinal Domenico Grimani, and a few of the scenes in the Farnese Hours are copied from the Grimani Breviary (Item 55), which Clovio would have seen while it was in the library of Cardinal Grimani.

This is the single most famous manuscript of the Italian Renaissance, its fame assured by the detailed description of it by Giorgio Vasari in the second edition of his *Lives of the Painters* (1568). Vasari appears to have been especially impressed with Clovio's mastery of the art of perspective; he describes the manuscript as having been

> executed by Don Giulio in a period of nine years and required such study and labour that it would never be possible to pay for the work, regardless of the price, nor is it possible to see elsewhere any more strange and beautiful variety than there is in all its scenes. . . . Such a diversity of things infuses so much beauty into the work that it appears a thing divine and not human, and all the more because the colours and manner of painting have made the figures, buildings, and the landscapes recede and fade into the distance with all those considerations that perspective requires.... Thus we may say that Don Giulio has surpassed in this field both the

> ancients and the moderns, and that he has been in our times a new, if smaller, Michelangelo. (Vasari, qtd. in Alexander 246)

Further, according to Vasari, Clovio was very proud of the manuscript, and in his old age "took great delight in showing it to visitors [to the Farnese Palace], an act recorded in El Greco's portrait of him in Naples" (Alexander 247).

The opening on display (ff. 72v–73r) shows the text of the Litanies. While Litanies are rarely illustrated in other Books of Hours, Clovio has chosen to represent here a Corpus Christi procession in the city of Rome, winding between the Castel Sant' Angelo on the right to (old) St. Peter's Cathedral on the left, with the throngs of Heaven rejoicing overhead. At the head of the procession, carrying the elements of the Sacrament, is Pope Paul III.

A second opening (ff. 17v–18r) is also shown, being the opening of the Office of Lauds in the Hours of the Virgin. On the left is the image of the Visitation of Mary to Elizabeth, which is the standard subject at this point in a Book of Hours. This Visitation is somewhat unusual in that in the landscape behind the women are the hills of ancient Rome. The image on the facing page shows two of the Four Daughters of God (an allegory of the "Virtues Reconciled," based on a verse of Psalm 84:11 ["Mercy and truth have met each other: justice and peace have kissed" (Douay-Rheims version)]): here we see Justice and Peace kiss each other. In the background is a pagan temple, perhaps to represent the "old dispensation" prior to the Incarnation. The female figures are accompanied by naked putti, etc.

The juxtaposition of the Visitation and the Four Daughters is original to Clovio, but has a certain appropriateness, not only in the way that the two scenes of meeting parallel one another, but also because both are associated with the Nativity: Mary visits Elizabeth after learning that she is to give birth to the Son of God, and the reconciliation of the Virtues was associated with the Nativity in that, after this Reconciliation, Gabriel was sent to the Virgin to tell her of her role in the birth of the Messiah (i.e., the Reconciliation of the Daughters of God was necessary before the Incarnation could take place).

In the margins are drawings of various figures in imitation of classical statues; lilies (floral emblem of the Virgin) appear in vases; the "Virgin with Unicorn" motif appears four times along the bottom. This is based upon Bestiary accounts of the way to capture a Unicorn (for which one needs a virgin), which was allegorized as a reference to the Incarnation: the Unicorn who is Christ submits to being captured by a Virgin, Mary. In the oval cameo at the bottom of the left-hand page is Presentation of the Virgin in the Temple; in the cameo on the right-hand page is her marriage to Joseph. ✲

Alexander, Jonathan J.G. *The Painted Page: Italian Renaissance Book Illumination, 1450–1550*. Munich and New York: Prestel Verlag, 1994. 246–48 (Item 132).

61. John Speed. *Theatrum imperii Magnae Britanniae* (1616)

Paper; printed from engraved plates; a limited number of copies were coloured (by hand); 51.0 x 38.0 cm.

Facsimile on display: Speed, John. *The Counties of Britain: A Tudor Atlas*. Intro. Nigel Nicolson. County commentaries by Alasdair Hawkyard. London and New York: Thames and Hudson, in association with the British Library, 1989.

JOHN SPEED'S *Theatrum imperii Magnae Britanniae* of 1616 (STC 23044), the basis for this facsimile, is a Latin translation of his English *The Theatre of the Empire of Great Britaine* of 1611 (STC 23041), which was reissued in a variety of reprints and new editions for the next century. The *Theatre* was intended (as is indicated by the fact that the two books share continuous pagination) as a companion volume to Speed's *The History of Great Britaine Under the Conquests of ye Romans, Saxons, Danes and Normans* (STC 23045). Both the *Theatre* and the *Theatrum* were printed in four volumes, and consisted of 67 double-page maps, primarily of the counties of England and the regions of Wales, Scotland, and Ireland. Many of the county maps include insets showing the street layout of major towns. On the verso of each map is a page of topographical, administrative, and historical information.

As Nigel Nicolson indicates in his Introduction, Speed intended to make each map "descriptive, useful, and a pleasure to look at. It could be a traveller's guide, or used for administrative purposes in an office — the boundaries of the hundreds, the units of local government, deer-parks, and estates, are all carefully marked — or it could be kept in a private library, where it was a way of travelling in imagination without expense or fatigue" (7). Curiously, the maps do not show roads, so they are of little use in peregrination, but are quite accurate in showing the positions of towns and villages relative to one another.

We show the map of Ireland (pp. 270–71). One does not need to go to Africa or Asia to find exotic creatures: just across the Irish Sea one can see "Wild Irish Folk" in their native habitat. The map was prepared around 1611, when English control over Ireland was at its most complete. ✻

Skelton, R.A. *County Atlases of the British Isles, 1579–1850: A Bibliography*. London: Carta Press, 1970. Items 7, 10, 11, 14, 16, and 18.

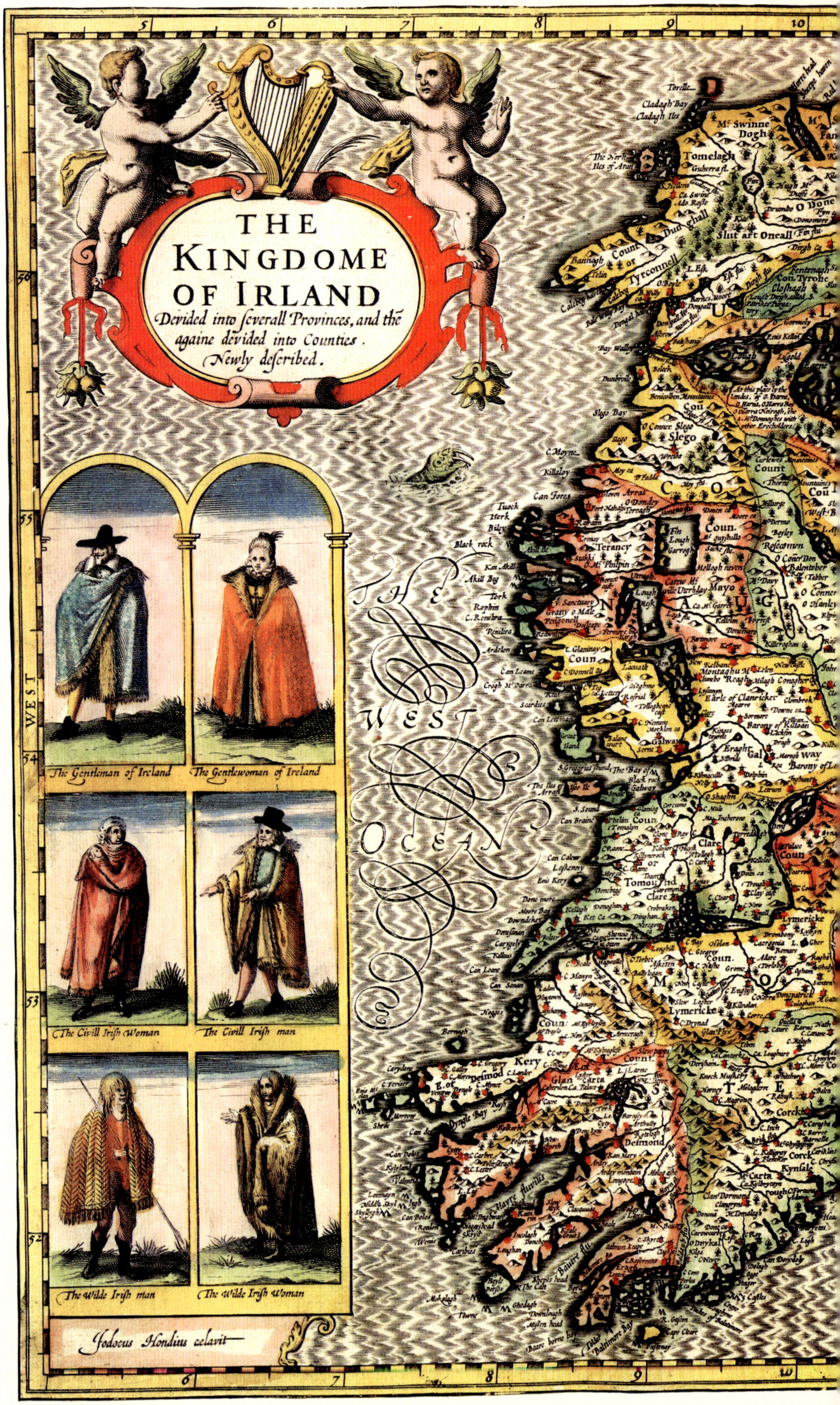
THE
KINGDOME
OF IRLAND
Devided into severall Provinces, and the againe devided into Counties. Newly described.
The Gentleman of Ireland
The Gentlewoman of Ireland
The Civill Irish Woman
The Civill Irish man
The Wilde Irish man
The Wilde Irish Woman
Jodocus Hondius caelavit
THE WEST OCEAN

Fig. 22

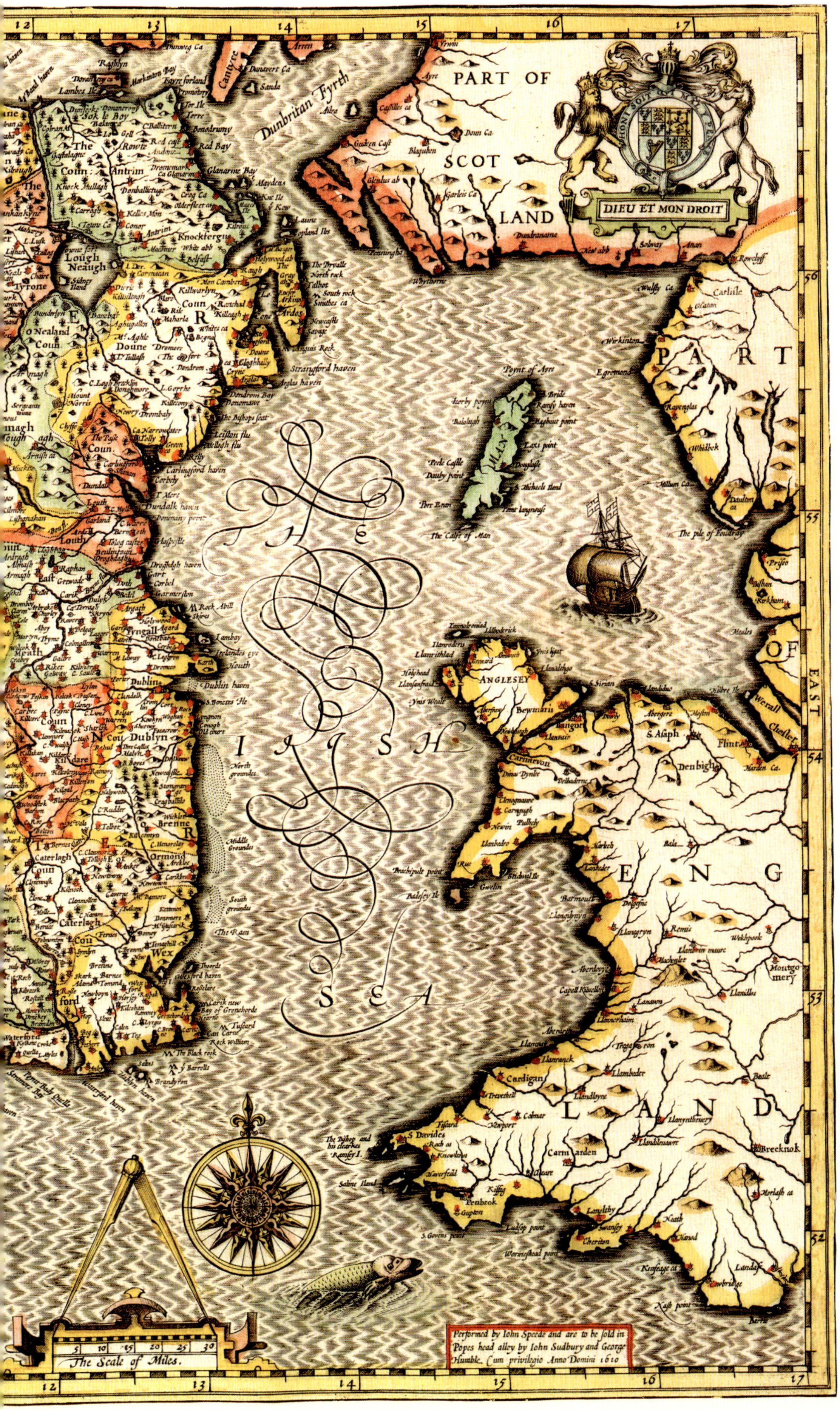
PART OF
SCOT
LAND
DIEU ET MON DROIT
Dunbritan Fyrth
PART
OF
EAST
ENG
LAND
THE
IRISH
SEA
ANGLESEY
Carlisle
Dublin
Dublyn
Antrim
Knockfergus
Lough Neaugh
Dundalk haven
Carlingford haven
Strangford haven
Dublin haven
Carnarvon
Bewmaris
Denbigh
Flint
S. Asaph
Mountgomery
Cardigan
Carmarden
S Davides
Penbrok
Breeknok
Poynt of Ayre
The Calfe of Man
The Scale of Miles
5 10 15 20 25 30
Performed by Iohn Speede and are to be sold in Popes head alley by Iohn Sudbury and George Humble. Cum privilegio Anno Domini 1610

62. The Coronelli Map of America

Produced in Venice in 1688.
Paper, printed from copperplate engraving.
Facsimile on display: new edition printed from a copperplate engraving by Zsolt Török.

VINCENZO CORONELLI (1650–1718) is perhaps best known for the production of early modern globes. He was the official cartographer to King Louis XIV of France, and produced mainly globes for the king before he returned to Venice in 1684 and founded a cosmographical society before becoming the official cosmographer of Venice.

The map shows the progress in depictions of America from the time of Sebastian Münster (Item 59), but still depicts California as an island and lacks much detail in the west and north. ✲

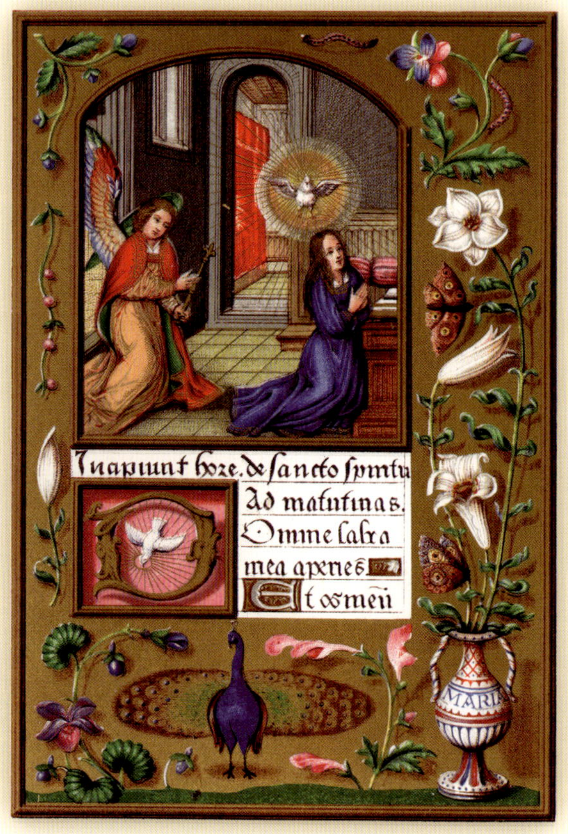

PRINTED in 11 and 12 pt. Emigre Mrs. Eaves, designed in 1996 by Zuzana Licko, and named for John Baskerville's housekeeper and, later, wife, Sarah Eaves; the font was selected for its medieval qualities, particularly its roundness and flourish. The headings are in Agedage Caroline (imitating a Caroline minuscule script) with Agedage Simple Versal; the initials and ornaments are selected from LTC Jacobean Initials and Bodoni Classic Ornaments. It is printed on Topkote Dull 100 lb text by McCallum Printing Group Inc. of Edmonton.

The design elements used in the catalogue but not otherwise identified are from the holdings of the Bruce Peel Special Collections Library: the Arenberg Book of Hours (Flemish, 1430s); *The Parables of Our Lord*, decorated by Henry Noel Humphreys (New York, 1849); and Henry Shaw, *The Art of Illumination as Practised During the Middle Ages* (London, 1870).

ISBN: 978-1-55195-187-4